FOUL DEEDS & SUSPICIOUS DEATHS IN GUILDFORD

FOUL DEEDS AND SUSPICIOUS DEATHS Series

Foul Deeds and Suspicious Deaths series explores in detail crimes of passion, brutal murders, grisly deeds and foul misdemeanours. From Victorian street crime, to more modern murder where passion, jealousy, or social deprivation brought unexpected violence to those involved. From mysterious death to murder and manslaughter, the books are a fascinating insight into not only those whose lives are forever captured by the suffering they endured, but also into the society that moulded and shaped their lives. Each book takes you on a journey into the darker and unknown side of the area.

Other titles in the series

Foul Deeds and Suspicious Deaths in Blackburn & Hyndburn, Steve Greenhalgh
ISBN: 1-903425-18-2. £9.99

Foul Deeds and Suspicious Deaths in and around Chesterfield, Geoffrey Sadler
ISBN: 1-903425-30-1. £9.99

More Foul Deeds and Suspicious Deaths in and around Chesterfield, Geoffrey Sadler
ISBN: 1-903425-68-9. £9.99

Foul Deeds and Suspicious Deaths in & around Durham, Maureen Anderson
ISBN: 1-903425-46-8. £9.99

Foul Deeds and Suspicious Deaths in and around Halifax, Stephen Wade
ISBN: 1-903425-45-X. £9.99

Foul Deeds and Suspicious Deaths in Leeds, David Goodman
ISBN: 1-903425-08-5. £9.99

Foul Deeds and Suspicious Deaths in Manchester, Martin Baggoley
ISBN: 1-903425-65-4. £9.99

Foul Deeds and Suspicious Deaths in Newcastle, Maureen Anderson
ISBN: 1-903425-34-4. £9.99

Foul Deeds and Suspicious Deaths in Nottingham, Kevin Turton
ISBN: 1-903425-35-2. £9.99

Foul Deeds and Suspicious Deaths around Pontefract and Castleford, Keith Henson
ISBN: 1-903425-54-9. £ 9.99

Foul Deeds and Suspicious Deaths in and around Rotherham, Kevin Turton
ISBN: 1-903425-27-1. £9.99

Foul Deeds and Suspicious Deaths Around the Tees, Maureen Anderson
ISBN: 1-903425-26-3. £9.99

More Foul Deeds and Suspicious Deaths in Wakefield, Kate Taylor
ISBN: 1-903425-48-4. £9.99

Foul Deeds and Suspicious Deaths in York, Keith Henson
ISBN: 1-903425-33-6. £9.99

Foul Deeds and Suspicious Deaths on the Yorkshire Coast, Alan Whitworth
ISBN: 1-903425-01-8. £9.99

Please contact us via any of the methods below for more information or a catalogue.
WHARNCLIFFE BOOKS
47 Church Street – Barnsley – South Yorkshire – S70 2AS
Tel: 01226 734555 – 734222 Fax: 01226 734438
E-mail: enquiries@pen-and-sword.co.uk –
Website: www.wharncliffebooks.co.uk

Foul Deeds & Suspicious Deaths in
GUILDFORD

CAROLINE MAXTON

Series Editor
Brian Elliott

Wharncliffe Books

Dedication

For My Father
The Inspiration

First Published in Great Britain in 2005 by
Wharncliffe Books
an imprint of
Pen and Sword Books Ltd.
47 Church Street
Barnsley
South Yorkshire
S70 2AS

Copyright © Caroline Maxton 2005

ISBN: 1-903425-78-6

Typeset in 11/13pt Plantin by Mac Style Ltd, Scarborough.

Printed and bound in England by
CPI UK.

Pen and Sword Books Ltd incorporates the Imprints of
Pen & Sword Aviation, Pen & Sword Maritime,
Pen & Sword Military, Wharncliffe Books,
Pen & Sword Select, Pen and Sword Military Classics
and Leo Cooper.

For a complete list of Pen & Sword titles please contact
PEN & SWORD BOOKS LIMITED
47 Church Street
Barnsley
South Yorkshire
S70 2BR
England
E-mail: enquiries@pen-and-sword.co.uk
Website: www.pen-and-sword.co.uk

Contents

Acknowledgements

A book of this sort requires a huge amount of research and I am very much indebted to the staff of the following libraries, archives and museums: the National Archives, The British Library, The British Library Newspaper Archives, The Surrey Police Archives at Mount Browne, the Museums of Farnham, Godalming and Guildford, but especially to the staff of the Surrey History Centre for always taking the trouble to find an answer, no matter how strange the question.

There are also many individuals whose contribution has meant a great deal to me. Firstly my thanks must go to Sam Milner for supplying the photographs of Guildford and the surrounding areas, and most especially for finding the grave of Emily Joy: to Mary and Richard Mobbs, Norah Adams and Judy-Ann Cook for putting time and thought into reading every chapter, when really they had better things to do: to Dr Malcolm Cooper for advice and for saving me from some truly embarrassing errors: to Philip Hutchinson, not only for putting me on the trail of Christopher Slaughterford, but for raising more than a few smiles on a ghost tour of Guildford, and last, but certainly not least, to Nicola Milne-Leith, whose enthusiasm for the research very nearly topped my own.

Introduction

T hankfully few of us encounter the realities of murder and serious violence in our lives, but most of us nevertheless feel drawn to understand the course of events that led other, less fortunate, people to their untimely end. And the motivation for this interest cannot be written off simply as a ghoulish preoccupation. If we learn the mistakes of the past then we are better prepared to avoid their repetition in the future. And so it is with the more unpleasant side of human nature; if we can learn to recognise those situations that might lead us into danger, to understand the qualities in others that might expose us to violence, to identify those pressures that provoke ordinary people to extraordinary acts of wickedness, then perhaps we are better prepared to deal with our own precarious moments in life.

In *Foul Deeds and Suspicious Deaths in Guildford* we find a wide range of personal histories that reflect the full spectrum of human behaviour. Some will provoke anger or outrage,

Guildford Guildhall seen from The Tunsgate. Guildford Museum

others sympathy and sadness. They all give an insight into life
and attitudes in the past, and the locations of the events will
be familiar to anyone living in or around Guildford.

As a major centre of commerce even from early times,
Guildford was equipped to deal with law-breakers from a wide
catchment area. It boasted a prison of sorts for over six
centuries, starting with several rooms in the keep of the King's
Castle in the thirteenth century. Prisoners were brought here
from as far afield as Sussex, and the Constables were regularly
petitioning for more secure fortifications. In 1343 one prisoner

Guildford House of Correction 1839. Surrey Advertiser and Surrey Times

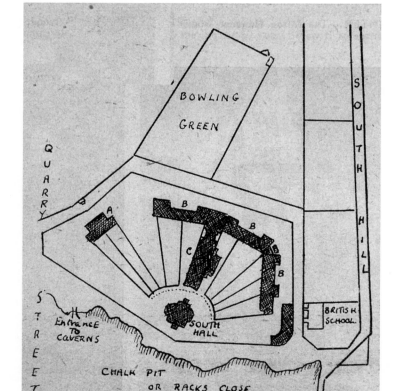

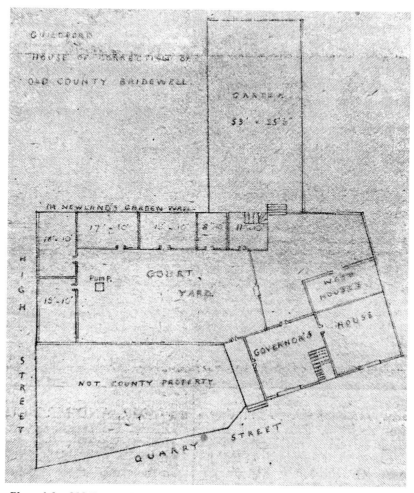

Plan of the Old County Bridewell. Surrey Advertiser and Surrey Times

did manage to escape and the unfortunate Constable of the Castle was fined £5, no small amount in those times.

Surrey acquired two new prisons in the course of the sixteenth century, Marshalsea and the White Lion in Southwark, and the King's Castle was no longer needed to house prisoners. But between the seventeenth and nineteenth centuries three successive houses of correction were constructed in Guildford, in the High Street, in Quarry Street and in South Hill. They all came under the control of the Justices of the Peace for the county of Surrey.

Public executions were an accepted facet of life in centuries past, and entire families, including children, were encouraged to attend. They were believed to serve as a powerful deterrent not only for hardened criminals but also for those skirting on the edge of criminality, and in chapter nineteen we see this aspect of capital punishment in its most extreme form: gibbeting. Church bells would toll to announce the start of the executioner's procession, just to be sure that no one missed it. In the latter half of the eighteenth century, it was estimated that one convict in five was sentenced to death, and not just for murder but for a series of lesser crimes ranging from highway robbery to forgery.

In chapter ten we catch a glimpse of the final days of two condemned men. Although all prisoners sentenced to death were routinely held in chains to prevent escape, they were permitted visitors, and in the case of George Chennell and William Chalcraft we can almost feel sorry for the two murderers as they bid their families a final farewell. The story is typical of its time in that the executions took place near the scene of the crime, and in this case the convicts' bodies were returned to the very house where the murders were committed. The dissection of the bodies by local surgeons and their exposure to public view may seem unnecessarily gruesome to us, but this practice can be traced back to the time of Henry VIII. It was only permissible, though, to carry out the procedure on the bodies of those convicted of murder, however much students of anatomy tried to get access to the bodies of those executed for other crimes.

The histories in this book cover a wide time span, the earliest taking place in the eleventh century, the others stretching forward into the mid-twentieth century. We see a noticeable change over this time in the methods of policing. In the story of the Unknown Sailor in 1786 it is left to a posse of local men to track down the villains, and it was in the last part of the eighteenth century and the beginning of the nineteenth that the need for more structure in law enforcement was recognised. We have all heard of the famous Bow Street

Portrait of J H Law, a Guildford Policeman. Surrey History Centre

Portrait of Sutton, a Guildford Policeman. Surrey History Centre

Portrait of Davis, a Guildford Policeman. Surrey History Centre

Portrait of Titley, a Guildford Policeman. Surrey History Centre

Crown Court, Godalming. Surrey History Centre

Runners, London thief-takers paid by a system of rewards, and London continued to lead the way in policing methods. It was 1829 when Peel's Metropolitan Police first took to the streets of the capital, and 1835 when Guildford and Godalming set up their own forces. The culprits responsible for the death of the vicar of Frimley in 1850 were tracked down thanks to the tenacious efforts of the first Head Constable of Godalming, William Biddlecombe.

We see, too, the advances made in forensic science and the nineteenth century cases strike today's reader as particularly basic in this respect. In chapter four we read of the frustrated complaints of the Coroner in 1904, when crowds of spectators trod over footprints at the scene of the murder of George White, destroying the only physical evidence that might have linked the murderer to his victim. And the case of the wigwam girl in chapter thirteen marked a turning point in the uses of forensic science to reconstruct the last moments of a victim's life.

The twenty-two cases described in this book are varied in both nature and context. And, hopefully, they give an insight into a great deal more than simply man's inhumanity to man.

CHAPTER 1

Until Death Do Us Part: The Murder of Emily Joy 1889

... a madness overtook him.

The funeral of nineteen-year-old Emily Joy was an emotional testimony to how well the young girl had been loved in her lifetime. The date was Monday 14 January 1889 and the day was suitably overcast and gloomy. Between three and four thousand mourners gathered at the cemetery in Godalming, and although police were on hand to ensure that the crowd behaved with suitable decorum, their presence was unnecessary. The mood was sombre, and the mother and siblings of the dead girl could barely contain their grief. For several days a constant stream of friends and acquaintances had been calling at the family home to view the body and pay their last respects; indeed the queue of mourners continued until just two hours before the funeral was due to start. The coffin, draped in a black velvet pall and laden with wreaths, was carried to the chapel in a hearse accompanied by three carriages. The expense of such a funeral was beyond the means of the Joy family, but friends and neighbours, under the direction of Mr Jearum, the stationmaster for whom Mrs Joy worked, had made a collection to ensure that Emily was given the funeral she deserved. As her coffin was lowered into the ground, her mother, her brother James and her sisters Mary Ann and Elizabeth moved forward to say their last farewell. Elizabeth became almost hysterical and had to be led away from her sister's newly dug grave.

There was one notable absence from the funeral however: Emily's fiancé Ebenezer Jenkins. But his absence was not voluntary; he was being held in custody charged with her murder.

Church Road, today known as Kings Road, where the Joy family lived. Sam Milner

It is undeniable that love and even lust are powerful emotions, but it is nevertheless difficult to understand the reason for Emily Joy's murder. She lived in Church Road, Farncombe, less than four miles from Guildford, with her widowed mother, Mary Ann Joy. Emily was a quiet, attractive, home-loving girl who was not only a companion to her mother, but provided her with practical and financial support too. Mindful of this fact the jury at Emily's inquest donated their fees to Mrs Joy.

Emily had met twenty-year-old Ebenezer Jenkins the previous year, and by August they had decided to become engaged. Jenkins was an artist who worked under his mother's maiden name of Wheatcroft, and he rented a studio close to Godalming High Street. The studio was a summerhouse in the garden of a Mr Harrison and it gave the artist the natural light he needed for his work, which mainly consisted of painting scenery for small touring theatrical companies. The studio was also entirely private and secluded.

Mrs Joy showed the natural concerns of a parent that her daughter should marry suitably. She therefore asked Jenkins to show that he could support Emily on his artist's salary and this he willingly did. He told Mrs Joy about his good connections with respectable families in Dorking, that he earned £1 a week from his work and that he expected to earn £2 a week before they were married. He also assured her that when he reached the age of thirty he would receive a considerable sum of

St John's Street, Farncombe. 'Godalming in Old Picture Postcards'

money, and that he expected £300 before the end of February. A telegram, apparently from the bank, was sent to Jenkins at the Joy's address confirming that £300 would be due on 25 February. On Christmas Day 1888 Ebenezer wrote a letter formalising his good intentions. It read:

High Street, Godalming, 1910. Godalming Museum, previously published in R Head 'Godalming in Old Picture Postcards'

I, the undersigned, agree to marry Miss Emily Joy at any time she may state. And I can further state that I, the undersigned, am in a position to marry, and that I have a standing income beside my small capital, which amounts to £500 10s, and that I swear I will never give the said Miss Joy any reason to complain or any unhappiness. I further state that when I reach the age of thirty that I have an amount in cash, namely £600, which I shall receive in quarterly payments. I have no further capital. I will also state that since I have been with the said Miss Joy I have never been in company with any young lady, and that I have never in my life committed any offence upon any young lady, and that I was never married during my past life, and I agree to make said young lady happy all her life. All I have stated I will swear on oath.

The need to confirm that he had never committed an offence on any young lady may strike us as odd, but as the two young lovers showed obvious and deep affection for each other, and in all ways, Jenkins appeared to treat Emily with kindness and consideration, Mrs Joy gave her blessing to the union and the date for the marriage was set for 15 March.

However, certain things gradually came to light to cause Mrs Joy to reconsider her decision. The first was that Jenkins always appeared to be short of cash, and borrowed from Emily who gave whatever she had quite freely. Mrs Joy was also unsettled by the fact that she did not know exactly where Jenkins lived and that he was very reluctant to talk about his parents. When he did mention his upbringing, his stories were not always consistent. At one time he even implied that he had been adopted. And it later emerged that his so-called good connections in Dorking were non-existent. Mrs Joy began to think she should withdraw her consent, but in the face of the couple's obvious attachment to each other she did not forbid them to meet. In fact, in the week before the murder, Jenkins stayed in the Joy's home.

There was other information that did not come to light until the trial, such as the fact that the telegram from the bank had been sent by Jenkins himself to fool the family into believing that he was due to receive money. Also Jenkin's career as an artist had only been of very recent duration. Before that he had tried his hand at various occupations, such as working as an insurance collector, setting up a shop selling electrical supplies and even starting up a band; but all his ventures seemed to be unsuccessful. He had had a close relationship with another young lady in Dorking, but there was nothing known about his past to suggest violence or aggression.

On the evening of the murder, Monday, 7 January 1889, Jenkins asked Emily to accompany him to his studio. Under normal circumstances she would not have agreed to go alone with her fiancé to such a private place, but he assured her it was to meet a Mrs Elliott from the Catteshall Coffee Tavern. She owed him £14, money that Jenkins in turn owed to Emily, and Mrs Elliott, he claimed, would only hand over the cash to the young lady herself. Needless to say, Mrs Elliott's visit was entirely fictitious; it was nothing more than a ruse to get Emily alone. At his trial Jenkins vigorously denied any intention to murder, but he did admit to having planned a seduction.

Arm in arm on their way to the studio the couple passed PC Steele, an officer from the Crown Pits Station, and he noted that they were talking happily together. Jenkins wished the

Cattashall Coffee Tavern (later spelt Catteshall), Farncombe. R Head 'Godalming in Old Picture Postcards'

Crownpits, Godalming. R Head 'Godalming in Old Picture Postcards'

police officer a good evening as they walked by. There was nothing in his demeanour to arouse suspicion.

Once in the studio, Jenkins asked Emily to look over the financial papers. Whilst she was reading he asked her whether she loved him, and she replied that yes, she did. At this moment, he later said, a madness overtook him. Perhaps he felt that if she loved him she should be willing to demonstrate this by agreeing to intercourse with him, but she evidently

Studio where Emily Joy was murdered. Godalming Museum

struggled and Jenkins dealt her a blow across the face, breaking her nose and leaving her semi-conscious. It was then that he raped her. As she regained full consciousness, he must have panicked at the extent of his assault on Emily. She was a respectable young lady, and would certainly not have overlooked such a violation. Jenkins must have been desperate to save himself from the consequences of his actions. His love for her seems to have been forgotten as he took the fur boa that Emily was wearing and wound it round her face and neck. He stuffed her silk handkerchief into her mouth and strangled her. He claims she said, 'Goodbye my darling; I am dying,' but this must surely have been a flight of fancy on Jenkins' part. He straightened her clothing, removed a jubilee half crown that she had been wearing as a brooch, turned her on her side and left, locking the studio door behind him.

Close-up of Jenkins' studio. Godalming Museum

Sadly Emily's muffled cries and struggles had been heard by a passer-by, but not recognised for what they were. Walter Ede, a butler who lived in nearby Carlos Road, passed within forty or fifty yards of the studio. As he walked towards the summerhouse he thought he heard two faint screams, but mistakenly assumed they had come from the direction of Latimer Road. As he got closer he heard a bumping sound, this time definitely coming from the studio, but he took no action.

As the evening wore on Mrs Joy became more and more concerned at Emily's absence. She was not the sort of girl to stay out late. At one o'clock in the morning Mrs Joy and her daughter Elizabeth walked the quarter of a mile from their home to Jenkins' studio but found it locked. They knocked on the door, and on hearing no response, lit a match to try to look through the keyhole. They could see nothing. They had no choice but to return home to wait for news, and this they received the following morning. In a letter which had been posted from Godalming that same day, Jenkins wrote:

Darling Mother – You will be deeply grieved to hear that Emmy and me are gone for ever. You will never see us again. We loved each other dearly, and swore we would never part. Dear mother, forgive me and her for all we have done, and let us be bearied [sic] together. Please do, in the same grave. So good-bye. For ever your loving son, E. S. W. Jenkins.

It is possible that Jenkins actually considered taking his own life after murdering his fiancée; in fact he considered various courses of action, judging from his conversations that night. At first he appeared calm. He went to the *Sun Inn* in Godalming, and ordered six pennyworth of brandy, for which he paid with the half crown taken from Emily's brooch. He chatted about the weather with a passing acquaintance, Arthur Singer, and then announced that he would soon be going far away, most likely to Egypt. Egypt was probably the most distant and exotic place Jenkins could think of, but since his current life was now in tatters, what did he have to lose? But remorse soon set in. He left the inn, his long cape trailing nearly to the ground behind him, and walked as he considered his situation.

Sun Inn *Godalming.* Sam Milner

Shortly before nine o'clock he met Harry Pennycot, a tanner, who worked in Godalming. Pennycot was a stranger to Jenkins but nevertheless the two walked together for a while in the direction of Witley. Jenkins asked him if he knew of any young ladies in the area, a question that Pennycot found odd. He said he knew nothing about any young ladies, at which Jenkins asked, 'Don't you think I am like a madman?' Now feeling uneasy, Pennycot assured him that he did not, to which Jenkins replied, 'I shall either come to the gallows, or else I shall drown myself.' He invited Pennycot to smoke a pipe with him but he declined. As the two men parted at Eashing Lane, Jenkins took off his cuff links and urged Pennycot to take them. Pennycot was reluctant but Jenkins insisted. The two men shook hands, and as he walked away, Jenkins called out, 'If anyone wants to know my name, it's Wheatcroft.' This was Jenkins' professional name. The fact that he had just given away his cuff links, probably the most valuable item he had on him, and the fact that he had made sure he could later be identified, may indicate that, at that particular moment, Jenkins did indeed intend to take his own life. Or perhaps he just wished to make it look as though did.

Between twelve and one o'clock on the day after the murder, Tuesday, 8 January, Jenkins went to the *Punch Bowl Inn* at Hindhead. He was in a very distressed state, and at times even crying. He ordered himself a glass of beer and the landlord, Augustus Sallis, asked him what was wrong. He told the barman a sorry tale. He said that he had made an agreement with his young lady that they would drown themselves together. 'She jumped over the railings into the river,' he explained, 'but I had not pluck enough to follow.' Mr Sallis asked whether Jenkins had made any attempts to rescue the young lady. Jenkins explained that he had felt paralysed and unable to do anything to save her, but that he wished to make a statement about it to the police. Mr Sallis had planned to go to Guildford that day on business and Jenkins asked if he could accompany him as far as the Borough Police Station. He wished to lay the whole affair before the police, he said. Mr Sallis agreed to this, especially as his wife did not wish to be left alone with Jenkins. On the way Jenkins may have changed his mind, because he told Mr Sallis he wished to leave to talk to an old friend. Suspecting that he might be trying to escape, Mr Sallis refused to allow him to leave, and Jenkins broke down and told the truth. He showed the landlord the marks on his hands where Emily had bitten him in the course of her struggles. 'I have told you lies,' he confessed. 'I murdered the girl myself; I strangled her.' Mr Sallis saw a police officer in Guildford High Street and was about to summon him over, but Jenkins begged to be spared the humiliation of being arrested in the street. He asked to be taken to the station instead, and this Mr Sallis agreed to do.

At the police station Jenkins calmly told a Sergeant Watts the whole story. He then broke down into uncontrollable sobs and said he hoped they would hang him.

Jenkins' distress was interpreted by most as being feigned, but this may not necessarily have been so. He had clearly vacillated about giving himself up to the authorities, and he did invent the story of the suicide pact, but he did also eventually confess. He might easily have made a bid to run away, if not to Egypt then at least to another part of Britain, but he did not. Guilt and remorse appear to have swept over him in waves, in between moments of formulating desperate plans to extricate himself from the dreadful situation he had created. During his time in custody before the trial he was kept under the supervision of a doctor in the infirmary, so apparently fragile was his mental state. During his trial at the County Assizes on Valentines Day 1889 his strange behaviour was noted by reporters. The *Surrey Advertiser* wrote:

> *He is a somewhat peculiar- looking young fellow. ... He had no collar, but a white scarf of "choker" character. He constantly muttered to himself, and smiled whilst smoothing his hair with his right hand, his somewhat idiotic expression being evidently assumed.*

Having been found guilty of murder by the jury, Jenkins was sentenced to death. The judge commented that he had, 'never known a crime committed under circumstances more shocking and more revolting.' He was to be hanged and buried within the precincts of the prison. He would not, as he had wished, be buried in the same grave as Emily.

Gravestone of Emily Joy. The inscription reads, 'No time for thought, no moment for a prayer, So swift was the spirit's violent flight.' Sam Milner

CHAPTER 2

A Knock-Kneed Case: The Deaths of Annie and Albert Keen
1932

Neighbours were baffled as to how this could have happened.

Keen Cottage, named after the family who had occupied it for at least three generations, lay in an isolated but picturesque spot on the edge of Cutt Mill Common. In 1932 it was occupied by Albert Keen and his wife Annie, and the couple, now aged sixty-one and fifty-four respectively, lived a quiet but contented existence. Attached to the cottage was a smallholding, and Albert cultivated this as his father had done before him. He also worked as a labourer for others in the neighbourhood. As a

Keen Cottage, Cutt Mill Common. Surrey Police Archives, Mount Browne

young man he had worked at Cutt Mill, at a time when the milling business was thriving under the ownership of a Mr Durrant. Later on he worked for Mr Nobes at Cutt Mill Farm, and then from the new year of 1932 as foremen cowman to Lady Guillemard at Rodsall Manor.

The Keens had married at Puttenham church twenty-five years previously. Annie, like Albert, had lived all her life at Cutt Mill, apart from a short period before her marriage when she worked as a domestic servant at Barton Lodge in Godalming. Her parents had lived in a small house on the common known simply as 'The Cottage.' Annie and Albert had no children, but they did have several cousins who visited regularly and they lived a full life tending their property and participating as active members of the village community.

The cottage itself was very secluded. It was sheltered by a tall, thick hedge that bordered the garden and this made it virtually invisible from the road across the common. The Keens made good use of their smallholding and it provided most of their daily needs. They had fruit from the trees that were grouped together in front of the house; there was a pigsty on one side of the garden gate and a chicken run on the other. At one time the Keens even kept their own cow, but now Albert collected a bottle of milk from work each day and brought it home in time for tea. There was an obvious affection between husband and wife and the two were known in the neighbourhood for their cheerful disposition.

On Friday, 7 October 1932 Albert finished his work slightly later than usual. At a quarter to six he took his bottle to Harry Green to be filled with milk and he put it in his rush basket to carry home. Lady Guillemard walked with him for the first fifty yards or so of his journey back to the cottage, and left him at the triangle of green by the entrance to the manor. His normal route home was along the rough cart track that ran by the Mill Pond; the mill itself had recently been demolished. Albert seemed in good spirits and chatted about how he would spend his forthcoming holiday from work. At about the same time Annie was getting their tea ready, having bid farewell to the workmen who were carrying out some structural renovations to the outside of the cottage and the shed that

DOUBLE MURDER CHARGE IN CUTT MILL TRAGEDY.

COUNSEL OUTLINES CASE FOR THE PROSECUTION.

ACCUSED'S EXPLANATION OF BLOOD STAINS.

MEDICAL EVIDENCE ILLUSTRATED BY TWO SKULLS.

A considerable queue awaited the opening of a special sitting of the Guildford County Bench on Thursday, when the case for the Crown against Godfrey Nobes (31), of Runfold, near Farnham, who is charged with the murder of Albert Keen at Cutt Mill and the wife, Mrs Annie Keen, at Gatwick Common, on October 7th, was opened. The Court sits at the Borough Hall.

he was working at a pork butcher's in Farnborough, and that he would be late.

EXAMINATION OF CLOTHING.

Mr. Paling then explained in detail the examination of the suit Nobes was wearing on October 7th, and said bloodstains had been found upon it. A number of places on the clothing had been analysed and tested, and the tests disclosed the presence of blood.

On the jacket were found 48 places each with human blood on them, 24 places on the

There was a severe wound in the throat and a quantity of blood around and on the floor. The door leading from the scullery to the cellar and the door leading to the kitchen were closed. He went into the living-room and drew up the blind, but did not touch anything else in the cottage. Later he returned to the cottage, and nothing had been touched so far as he could see.

On October 9th he went to Cutt Mill Pond about midday and found the stick (produced) floating in the water at the end of the wall on the north side of the pond. The heavy end of

Headline in the Surrey Advertiser. Surrey Advertiser

adjoined it. She had had a pleasant afternoon; her cousin had visited for a chat and Annie had walked with her part of the way home across the common. Now the table was laid ready for their meal and she made herself a cup of cocoa while she waited for Albert.

On the following morning, Saturday, 8 October, Robin Huber came to the cottage at about a quarter to eight in the morning. He did odd jobs about the place for Annie and helped Albert feed the animals on the smallholding. He found the back door open, and, as usual, called out to Mrs Keen to let her know he had arrived. But he was stopped short by the sight of her lying on the scullery floor, her skirt rucked up beneath her as though she had been dragged a little way, and around her body he saw a sizeable puddle of blood. He was understandably afraid to approach the body, and instead ran back home to inform his mother of the dreadful thing he had discovered. Mrs Huber came to the cottage straight away and the alarm was raised; the labourers who were working on Keen Cottage came to assist. One of them crawled through a hole in the cellar wall and made his way to the scullery. When he got there he found Mrs Keen, who only the day before had been

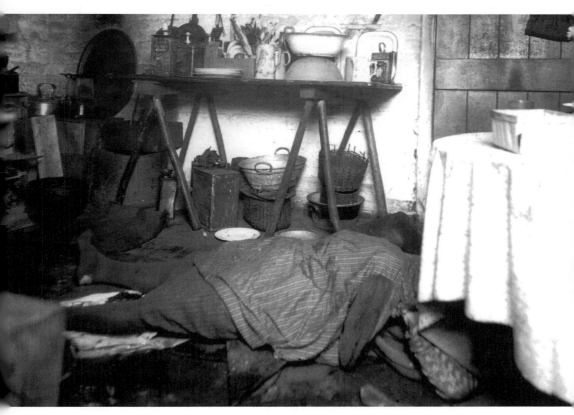

The body of Annie Keen in the scullery of Keen Cottage. Surrey Police Archives, Mount Browne

chatting to him over a cup of tea. Now she lay on the floor with a deep cut to her throat and an injury to her head. A large knife, normally to be seen hanging up in the kitchen, was found beneath the linoleum less than two feet from her body, and on the floor was a broken whetstone. A search was immediately launched for Albert. By now he had been missed at work at Rodsall Manor and Lady Guillemard had sent her chauffeur to Keen Cottage to investigate. It was not like Albert to be late for work, and it must be something very serious indeed to have prevented him from sending word to the house.

Albert Keen was found less than 300 yards from the cottage, submerged nine inches below the surface of the water and

The pond at Cutt Mill where Albert Keen's body was found. Surrey Police Archives, Mount Browne

standing in an upright position in Mill Pond. There was a noticeable wound to his forehead.

Neighbours were baffled as to how this could have happened. Had they both been murdered and if so by whom? Or had Albert murdered Annie then drowned himself in the pond, injuring his head as he fell on a nearby tree stump? The police were as bewildered as the inhabitants of Cutt Mill. Friends of the Keens immediately discounted the theory of murder and suicide; the couple were happy, healthy and clearly devoted to each other. But if they had both been murdered, what could the motive have been? At first glance the investigating police officers thought it was robbery, since every drawer in the house had been left open just a fraction. But neighbours explained that Annie always kept them like that; the house was damp and if she closed the drawers they got stuck and were very troublesome to open. There were two boxes wide open in the bedroom. Did Annie keep these open too, or were these signs that a burglar had been at work?

Further investigation did shed a little light on the mystery. The injuries to Albert's head were more extensive than at first thought, and floating near to the body was a hazel stick, about one inch in thickness and sharp at one end. On the edge of the pond near the track that Albert must have taken the previous day, was a brick tied with a piece of string. The police surgeon, Dr Milligan, felt that the wounds to Albert's head were consistent with having been caused by the corner of a brick and possibly also the stick. In his opinion they were more likely to have been inflicted before Albert entered the water, and further tests were being carried out in the hope of confirming this. It would seem, then, that the murder/suicide theory looked less likely. And to confirm this, Albert's rush basket that he took to work every day to carry his lunch and his milk bottle, was found on the bottom of the pond beside him. It looked very much as though Albert had not reached his home on the Friday evening, as the basket still contained the full bottle of milk.

The investigation widened. Police questioned locals and visitors about any small details they may have noticed on that Friday. Ernest Glew, of Worplesdon Road, Stoughton, was a bus driver for the Yellow Bus Services, and on Friday, 7 October he was working on a route between Farnham and Guildford. He remembered picking up a passenger, later identified as Godfrey Nobes, who boarded at Sandy Cross and alighted at the Shoelands Crossroads shortly before four in the afternoon. He remembered Nobes because he did not have the money for the fare, but promised to pay it on his return journey. Glew did not see him again that day.

Norman Vessey was the gamekeeper for the Cutt Mill district, and on 7 October, a little after five fifteen in the afternoon, he was walking by the Cutt Mill pond towards the site where the old mill had stood. It was raining slightly and he saw someone walking by the pond. It was a man wearing a blue suit and a light grey trilby hat, but no mackintosh. Although he did not know Nobes by sight, he was later able to identify the man at Guildford police station and it turned out to be Godfrey Nobes. Nobes had asked him where he could find the nearest bus stop for Guildford, a slightly unusual question for someone who had lived most of his life in Cutt Mill. The Nobes family home had been Cutt Mill Farm, where Albert had at one time worked for Godfrey's late father. Norman Vessey also said that later on the same afternoon he saw another man walking by the pond, and a third man with a cocker spaniel in a car parked at the corner. He watched them for about a quarter of an hour because he suspected them of poaching. At the end of that time the man who had been by the pond got into the car and the two men drove off.

The police felt it was time to question Nobes about his activities on 7 October. Cutt Mill Farm now stood empty, and Godfrey Nobes was living at the *Princess Royal* public house in Runfold. The pub was run by a Mrs Annie Hook, and since Nobes was engaged to Mrs Hook's daughter, Gladys, at the time, the arrangement was that Nobes would live with the family and pay 12s 6d a week for his food and lodgings. Godfrey was falling behind with the payment of his rent, and at the time of the murder owed Mrs Hook £2 12s 6d. He managed to hide from them the fact that he was unemployed, telling the family that he had a job as a chauffeur and that he was training to be a butcher. He left the house each day and killed time until the evening in order to keep up the pretence.

When the police questioned him he made a full statement, revising it slightly when certain inconsistencies arose. He told them that on Friday, 7 October he left home, telling Gladys and Mrs Hook that he was working that day at a pork butcher's and that he would be late home. To pass the time he first walked to the *Bricklayers' Arms* in Farnham, then on to Aldershot, Ash and Tongham. He stopped to eat a crust of bread and cheese that he had brought with him before taking the bus at Sandy Cross to Shoelands. This took him to about half past four in the afternoon. He continued his statement:

> *I then walked over Puttenham Common towards Cutt Mill by way of Hillberry, arriving at Cutt Mill about 5.55pm, where I spoke to a keeper on the estate about the place in general. We parted about 6.15pm; the keeper went towards Puttenham Common, and I walked towards the Shakleford Road. I did not see anyone else*

until I got over Cutt Mill crossroads on the Seale-Farnham road,
where I saw the keeper again go down his own drive to the road.

He said he sheltered from the rain for about three-quarters of an hour and then continued along the Farnham road where he twisted his ankle, forcing him to rest for a while longer. He arrived home, quite wet from the rain, at about ten o'clock, had his supper and went straight to bed. As he signed the statement, he said, 'That's right. That's all I know.'

Nobes' clothes were taken for examination; there were what appeared to be blood stains on his suit and on his hat. Dr Gerald Roche Lynch, director of chemical pathology at St Mary's, London, carried out a more thorough investigation, although forensic tests in the 1930s were limited in comparison to those of today. He found that the suit, at least, had been washed, but the coat still tested positive for blood in forty-eight places and twenty-four on the waistcoat and trousers, although it was not sufficient for him to say categorically that it was human blood, except in three places. Further stains, apparently of blood, were found on a hat, a handkerchief, a small stain on a shirt, and on the sleeve of a pullover. Nobes said that he suffered from frequent nose bleeds, something that was confirmed by Mrs Hook, and that if the stains were indeed blood, they were most likely either from this cause or from animals, such as rabbits, that he had killed.

He openly admitted that he knew the Keens, and that he had visited them the previous week to discuss the purchase of some geese. He did not deny that he had been in the area at the time of the murders, but said that he knew nothing about them.

The police were now beginning to formulate a theory. The notion that Albert might have killed Annie before drowning himself had now been set aside; the police were convinced that they were dealing with a case of double murder. They felt it most likely that Albert had been attacked first as he returned home from work. Any signs of a struggle between him and his assailant would have been washed away by the heavy rainfall of that Friday night. The attacker must have been familiar with

Albert's normal routine, they felt, and was waiting in hiding for him to pass on his usual route home. Albert must then have been rendered unconscious by one of the blows to his head. In the opinion of the pathologist, the blow to his forehead would have been sufficient to knock him out. He was then thrown into Mill Pond, along with the basket that he was carrying, and further blows were administered to the top of his head while he was in the water. Having made sure that Albert was not going to disturb him, the murderer then went to Keen Cottage. He hit Annie first with the whetstone that was later found on the floor spattered with blood. While she lay unconscious he went upstairs to force open the boxes in the bedroom in the hope of finding cash or other items of value. Albert and Annie refused to use a bank for their savings; indeed Albert had not used a bank since 1902. Anyone who was aware of this fact might have expected to find a considerable sum of money hidden away somewhere. It is impossible to say for sure exactly what was missing from the boxes. But why did he kill Annie rather than just leave her unconscious? Did she regain consciousness as he was returning downstairs? Did she recognise her attacker? She would, of course, have been totally unaware of what had befallen Albert, but if she recognised the man who had hit her on the head, it would not take the police long to piece the story together. From the way the blood lay in relation to the body it seemed as though her throat had been cut as she lay on the floor. So it would seem that the murderer picked up the large knife hanging in the kitchen and cut Annie's throat using a stabbing and slicing motion, just as butchers would use to slaughter a sheep.

No information had been forthcoming about the two other men seen by the gamekeeper. But in the light of all the evidence, including the blood on Nobes' clothing, the police were convinced that they had found their man. They arrested Godfrey Nobes and he was charged with the murder of Albert and Annie Keen before the magistrates at Guildford.

At his Assize Court trial Nobes pleaded 'not guilty' to the charge. The evidence was put before the jury, although Nobes himself did not take the stand; he merely made the following statement to the jury:

Ladies and Gentlemen. I am not guilty of either of these murders. When I was arrested by the police, I told them everything I knew, and everything I said is true.

His counsel, Mr Manley, pointed out to the jury that there was no way to ascertain the age of the stains on Nobes' clothing, and he reminded them that until recently he had been working as a farmer, so that they might well expect to find spots of animal blood on his clothing. The only three stains proven to be of human blood could be explained by the frequent nosebleeds suffered by Mr Nobes. He accused the police of being single-minded in their pursuit of Nobes, and of failing to pursue other possibilities. 'Their noses,' he said, 'were so hot on the trail that they could look neither to the right nor to the left.' He placed a few of the possibilities before the jury. He did not discount the possibility of murder and suicide rather than a double murder; he put forward the theory that the men seen in the car may have been responsible, and even made a passing reference to a sister of Albert's who had previously lived with them, and who was mentally unstable. Despite the valiant efforts of the prosecution to prove otherwise, it was, in his view, 'a rotten, weak and knock-kneed case'. It was enough to sow the seed of doubt.

In his summing up, the judge, Mr Justice Hawke, pointed out that Nobes had declined to take the stand himself; he did not comment on the significance of this, but warned the jury that unless they were satisfied beyond all reasonable doubt, they should acquit Godfrey Nobes. And acquit him they did.

The little parish church at Puttenham, where Annie and Albert had been married twenty-five years earlier, was filled to overflowing for their funeral. Family, friends and neighbours watched as the two coffins, covered with flowers, were placed side-by-side in front of the steps of the chancel. Sir Laurence Guillemard read the lesson and the rector, the Reverend Power, conducted the service. And so, on Friday, 14 October 1932, Annie and Albert were laid to rest together, buried in the same grave. The mystery of their deaths remains unsolved in the eyes of the world.

CHAPTER 3

CHAPTER 3

The Baby in the Canal:
The Case of Clifton Derigo
1924

He was fully clothed and perfectly formed, and although the rescue team tried artificial respiration he could not be saved.

At eight o'clock in the evening, just three days before Christmas 1924, Henry West heard screams coming from the lock near his home in St John's, Woking. He went to the bridge overlooking the Basingstoke Canal and met a man named Frederick Brown, who had also heard the cries of a woman coming from the direction of the canal. They turned the light on Brown's bicycle towards the bushes along the towpath but saw nothing. A few moments later they heard a woman's voice calling for help and realised that the sound was coming from the water. Looking towards Penley's Lock they saw a woman clinging to the iron bars of the lock gate; she was half submerged in the water but had managed to raise her upper body out of the water by hanging on to the gate.

Headlines in the Surrey Advertiser.
Surrey Advertiser

WOKING MURDER CHARGE REDUCED.

PLEA OF INFANTICIDE ACCEPTED.

WOMAN WHO THREW BABY INTO CANAL BOUND OVER.

Flora Cecilia Derigo (24), servant, was indicted at Surrey Assizes on Wednesday for the murder of Martin Derigo, at 1924. She pleaded guilty to infanticide and she was bound.

Mr. H. H. Trustor of Public Prosecution, and Mr. Trusted said war, prisoner m shortly afterward not follow, and i acquainted with lived together as ton. In August, tion at Woking, the house of Mrs John's, Woking, was no doubt Si proper preparation arrival, and the it. Smith seemed at that time, and saying he had go porary job, and was unable to s

WOKING MURDER CHARGE

YOUNG MOTHER COMMITTED FOR TRIAL.

ALLEGED ADMISSIONS CONCERNING BABY'S DEATH.

The hearing of the Woking murder charge was carried a stage further on Monday, when the magistrates committed Flora Cecilia Derigo to the next Surrey Assizes on a charge of murdering her baby by throwing it into the Basingstoke Canal at St. John's on Dec. 22nd.

The accused woman, looking flushed, but otherwise composed in bearing, listened quietly to the evidence. The man Smith, the father of the child, who had been provided with a seat in the hall of the police-station prior to the resumption of the hearing, was the second witness. He appeared pale and ill, but gave evidence in a firm voice.

The magistrates present were Mr. Alfred Brown (chairman), Mr. J. Hutchinson Driver and Miss D. C. Egerton.

CASE FOR PROSECUTION

Basingstoke Canal at St John's. Sam Milner

They pulled her out and guided her to a seat but she remained distressed. 'My baby,' was all she could say, 'my baby's in there,' pointing to the canal. The men peered into the dark water but nothing was visible. As they continued searching they asked the young woman how the baby had ended up in the canal. 'I threw it in,' she replied, 'I chucked it in in a fit of temper.'

A doctor and the police were called. As the canal was being dragged Henry West walked the young mother up and down the towpath in an effort to calm her down, and one hour later the body of a baby boy was found. He was fully clothed and perfectly formed, and although the rescue team tried artificial respiration he could not be saved.

At Knaphill police station twenty-four-year-old Flora Derigo told her story. She lived with the baby's father, Sidney Smith, in two rooms in the house of a Mrs Martin, at The Orchard, St John's, Woking. She went by the name of Mrs Smith although they were not in fact married to each other; they each had a spouse still living. Flora's husband was an American soldier she had met and married during the First World War, and although the soldier had made all the

Bridge over the Basingstoke Canal at St John's. Sam Milner

necessary travel arrangements for Flora to join him, her brother had intervened and prevented her from leaving the country and her family. In August 1923 she met Sidney Smith and by the new year of 1924 the two were living together. Their son, Clifton Barrington Martin Derigo, was born on 13 November and was under six weeks old when he met his death.

Smith and Derigo had only moved to Woking in September of that year, after Smith found employment there; he described his occupation as 'decorative artist'. Neighbours said that the couple made all the proper preparation for the arrival of the child, and that after the birth Flora seemed very attached to her baby. Difficulties arose when Smith apparently lost his job, and the couple were heard to argue on more than one occasion. Smith claimed that Flora altered in the month

Lock gate at St John's. Sam Milner

before the birth, becoming jealous and tearful, and in his words, 'rather given to hysteria'.

On 18 December Sidney Smith walked out of the house in The Orchard, leaving nothing more than a brief note for Flora. In it he said he was going to Southampton to look for work, and that he would send her some money as soon as he possibly could. Flora assumed she had been abandoned. She waited for four days and heard nothing whatsoever, and with every passing day became more despondent. Their landlady, Mrs Martin, sat with Flora early in the afternoon of the baby's death. She recalled that the baby was asleep in his bassinette, but there were no blankets covering him; she suggested to Flora that he should be wrapped up or he would catch cold, and Flora, in the lethargy typical of depression, shrugged and said, 'It won't hurt.'

As well as coping with feelings of rejection and abandonment, Flora had practical issues to deal with. She had almost no money. In her purse was 1s 8d and she had no idea when, or even whether, she would hear from Sidney Smith again. She told police that, 'this man [Smith] left me without a pennypiece. I have no one to go to and no money. He said he would send for me, and I expected him back, but he has not written since he left last Thursday.' In her desperation she wrote to a Mr Berger regarding a sum of money that Smith was owed by an insurance company. In the letter she asks for £5 that Smith was expecting to receive and her tone perfectly reflects her vulnerability and desperation. She writes:

> *I am very worried as he has gone away to work, and I am anxiously waiting for the £5 to carry on with. He has assured me that it would be here this week, and as it has not arrived yet I have taken it upon myself to write and ask you if he has been paid out, or if it is due to him. Hoping you will pardon me writing to you, and trusting you will kindly oblige me with an early answer as I am very worried.*

She signed her name 'F C Smith'. The letter was never posted but was found in her handbag on the day of her son's death.

The inquest returned a verdict of wilful murder at the beginning of January 1925. The baby's father, Sidney Smith, sat in court looking pale and drawn as he listened to the evidence. When Frederick Brown, one of the two men who had rescued Flora from the canal, described how the mother had admitted throwing her baby into the water, Smith collapsed and was carried from the courtroom, apparently unconscious. He might have guessed that leaving home with only a brief note as explanation would distress Flora, but he could not have anticipated such devastating consequences, and he must have been profoundly aware of his part in the sequence of events that led to his son's death.

Flora Cecilia Derigo was committed for trial at the Surrey Assizes in March 1925.

She was reported as 'looking flushed, but otherwise composed in bearing'. The court accepted her plea of guilty to infanticide but not guilty to the charge of murder. She said that she had thrown her baby into the canal 'in a fit of madness' and that she had jumped in afterwards to try to rescue him. It was the opinion of Dr Morton of Holloway Prison that Flora had not fully recovered from the effects of childbirth at the time of the offence; this, added to the stress caused by Smith's departure, had resulted in mental instability. Flora's sister Constance, who lived in Brighton, said that she was willing to take her in and look after her.

In the light of all this the judge eventually decided against a custodial sentence and instead Flora was bound over in the sum of £50. His Lordship was at pains to point out that this in no way diminished the seriousness of the crime, but given the special circumstances and the fact that a home was now available to her, 'he was able to adopt the best course in the interests of justice and the prisoner in not sending her to prison.' Flora was fortunate to have come before a judge whose capacity for humanity and understanding was far ahead of its time.

CHAPTER 4

Foul and Dastardly Murder: The Death of an Edwardian Teenager 1904

The teenager lay on his back, his sightless eyes staring up at the sky.

The grounds of the Wrecclesham vicarage, thick with trees, sloped sharply down to the winding footpath used by the villagers. The path led from Fairthorn Terrace to River Row past a group of just six cottages. A high stone wall separated the vicarage from the path and if anyone had been able to peer through the darkness on the night of Sunday, 17 April 1904 they would have seen blood spattering that wall. On the footpath itself lay a sizeable pool of blood and twenty feet away, on the edge of a nearby hop plantation and hidden by nothing more than the darkness, was the body of sixteen-year-old George White.

Headline from the Surrey Advertiser. Surrey Advertiser

TERRIBLE TRAGEDY NEAR FARNHAM.

GROOM FOUND MURDERED AT WRECCLESHAM.

SHOCKING INJURIES — HEAD FRACTURED AND THROAT CUT.

ROBBERY THE MOTIVE.

MURDERER AT LARGE.

River Lane Wrecclesham. Frances Frith and Co

However, none of this was discovered until the early light of morning when a carter, who lived in one of the cottages, set out for work. His name was Thomas Stockham and he set off before six o'clock to make the usual journey to the home of his employer, Mr J Knight, in Farnham. He got no further than about thirty yards when he saw the pool of blood on the path. The nearby body was appallingly easy to see in the light of day, and Thomas, shocked at his discovery, called out to a neighbour, Alfred Blake, for assistance. The men quickly informed the police and a murder inquiry was immediately set in motion; from the state of George White's body, it was plain that his death had been no accident.

The teenager lay on his back, his sightless eyes staring up at the sky. Next to his body was a newly hewn hazel stick and it took no great leap of imagination to link the stick to the fracture on the young man's skull. By far the worst injury, though, was the slash to his throat. So deep were the four distinct cuts that they seemed to extend almost to the spinal column. Very little blood was visible at the spot where the body was found, and the logical conclusion was that George had been murdered on the footpath and his body then dragged the few yards off the walkway. George's trouser pockets were turned inside out, indicating to the police that robbery had been the motive for the murder, although the sum of eightpence halfpenny remained in the breast pocket of his jacket. Police decided to remove the body to the *Bear Inn*, Wrecclesham and news soon spread to the press who gave reports of the 'Foul and Dastardly Murder' in the following day's editions.

George White had lived in the area for at least three years and held a steady job as under-groom on the estate of Mr William Trimmer at Runwick. He lived with his brother Henry, who worked as coachman for Mr Trimmer, and with Henry's wife. The young man had a good reputation in the community; he was teetotal, well behaved and was never known to mix in dubious company. He attended the lads' class of the Wrecclesham night school, and was a member of the Bible Class. Little more could be expected of a sixteen-year-old boy.

On the evening of the murder, Sunday, 17 April 1904, George was seen picking a bunch of primroses from the copse near his home. Then at about six-thirty he walked into Farnham to post some letters for his master. George had clearly timed his journey with care, for at Farnham cemetery he was able to overtake Miss Phoebe Mepham, a nursery maid at Runwick House, herself returning home after attending the evening service at Farnham Parish Church. The primroses had found their intended destination. George offered to walk her

Runwick House, Wrecclesham.
The author

Stables at Runwick House Wrecclesham. The author

home, and the two ambled back with no great sense of urgency. Close to eight-thirty he left Phoebe at the wrought iron gates of Runwick House, telling her that he intended to go straight home to bed. It was a clear night and they had seen no one else on their walk. George left for his own home on the Trimmer estate and Phoebe watched him walk away, but as she went inside the house she was aware of the sound of other footsteps on the road behind him.

George, it seems, was not the only one with amorous inclinations towards Phoebe Mepham. A workmate, eighteen-year-old Frank Fry, had been following behind them at a cautious distance and was very unhappy with what he saw. On the path by the vicarage someone grabbed roughly at George, and if that person were indeed Frank, then as the taller and more muscular of the two he would have had the upper hand in the struggle. At that moment a Mrs Brewer, who was visiting her mother in River Row, passed by on her way to buy beer from Mrs Gates' shop on the corner of Fairthorn Terrace, and she noted the scuffle. The light by this time was insufficient for her to identify faces, but she noticed that both young men were respectably dressed, although from the way at least one of them was behaving, she assumed they were the worse for drink. One had hold of the other, she later said, and 'was leading, or rather, dragging, the other along'. As she walked by, the stronger of the two hauled the other out of her way saying, 'make room for a lady, mate.' Fearing that this was a drunken brawl and not wishing to get involved, she hurried past. As she left she heard the sound of a heavy fall and a scream. She called out, 'Is anyone hurt?' and got the simple response, 'No'. She called again and this time the reply sounded sharp and aggressive: 'I tell you no.' Despite then hearing a gurgling sound, she feared for her own safety, and walked swiftly on to the shop. On her way back she saw nothing, but heard scuffling noises in the nearby hop plantation and the sounds of heavy breathing.

George was not missed at home until five forty-five the following morning, when his brother Henry went into his room to wake him up for work. He found George's bed empty and no sign that it had been slept in. This was at about the same time that Thomas Stockham was making his discovery of George's body in the hop plantation by the vicarage. The previous night Henry and his wife had gone to bed leaving the door on the latch for George. He was a young man, after all, and they allowed him the freedom to come and go as he pleased. It was nothing unusual; but to find his bed empty and unused was rather more alarming. Henry's concern deepened and his worst fears were realised in a very short time. News of the discovery of the body on the edge of the plantation soon spread, and at seven o'clock Henry went to the scene of the murder to identify his brother's body. To him also fell the unenviable task of breaking the dreadful news to their father, who lived in Oakhanger, Hampshire. We can only imagine the anguish such news would have caused.

George's body remained at the *Bear Inn* until after the inquest on Wednesday, 20 April, when it was removed to his home on the Runwick estate. The funeral was held on Friday 22 in appropriately drizzly weather. Hundreds of people turned out to bid their final farewell to the sixteen-year-old,

The Bear Inn, *now known as* The Bear and Ragged Staff, *where George White's body lay before the inquest.* Sam Milner

and virtually every household in the neighbourhood kept its blinds drawn as a mark of respect. As well as members of the immediate family, George's workmates and the servants of Runwick gathered at the parish church. Among them would have been Phoebe Mepham.

Villagers clustered in groups along the roadside to watch the passing of the funeral bier, which was drawn by labourers from the estate. Someone had paid for a good quality coffin trimmed with brass fittings and a brass inscription that read simply, 'George White, died 17th April, 1904, aged 16 years'. Many of the villagers carried sprays of flowers to place at the graveside and as the procession reached the gates of the church a group of constables stood to attention and saluted the remains of the young man. Four labourers from the estate

The Parish Church at Wrecclesham. Sam Milner

carried the coffin into the church to the sound of sombre organ music provided by Mr Dawson, the parish organist. The vicar, Reverend C H Keable, conducted a moving service, although on the following Sunday he could not resist the temptation to use the death of the teenager as a warning to others who chose to walk out on a Sunday evening rather than attend his services. Given the apparently wholesome nature of this particular and unfortunate teenager, his sermon seemed both unnecessarily pompous and more than a little unfair. But he appears to have restrained his pomposity at the funeral itself and the general opinion was that it had been a memorable service. George's classmates from the Wrecclesham night school lined the pathway from the church door to the cemetery where George's grave had been carefully prepared with moss, ivy and a selection of spring flowers, including primroses.

Eighteen-year-old Frank Fry, cowman on the Runwick estate, was arrested on Tuesday, 19 April for the murder of his fellow worker, George White. Following information from witnesses who had seen Fry set off behind George and Phoebe on the night of the murder, and after finding bloodstains on

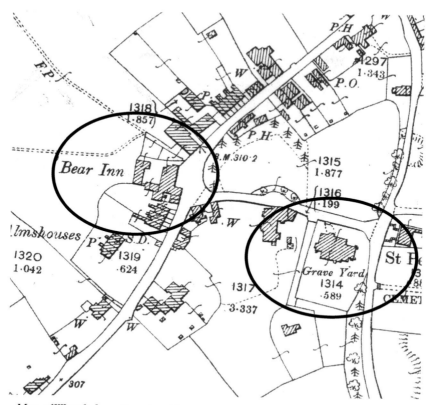

Map of Wrecclesham. Reproduced from 1897 Ordnance Survey Map

Fry's clothing and on his knife, the police felt sure they had found the right man. Jealousy was an obvious motive. He denied the charge and even threatened to cut his own throat given half the chance. When questioned about the stains on his Sunday best clothing he claimed the marks were from red paint. He did not account for the blood in the joints of his knife, nor for the fact that scour marks indicated that it had recently been vigorously scrubbed. A friend later gave evidence that Frank had had a nose bleed on the night of the murder, but if this was the source of the blood on his clothing, it is odd that Frank did not tell the police so himself.

At the inquest, the Coroner expressed his extreme frustration at the fact that so much evidence at the scene of the murder had been destroyed by the many onlookers, who had been walking around the area out of mere curiosity. Footprints, then a valuable source of evidence, had been damaged beyond use. The Coroner was also concerned at the way the case had been reported in the press. In his view, 'The grand idea with regard to the law that a person was considered innocent until he was proved to be guilty was very often abused and lost sight of.'

Fry was in a state of great agitation. There was evidence that strongly suggested his presence in the area of the crime. He had been seen following the young couple on the night of the murder, and a fellow employee, James Wilkinson was convinced he saw him that same evening at River Row. As he approached Fry, Wilkinson greeted him, although he says Fry declined to reply. At the time he thought this was strange, and asked him about it the following morning, but Fry claimed not to have been in the area at all. Added to this were the bloodstained clothes and the blood on the knife. It did not look good for him, and when under arrest at the police station he lit a cigarette, commenting, 'I suppose this may be my last one if they hang me.'

But the fates were kinder to Frank Fry than to George White. When the case came before the magistrates it was clear that one of two possibilities remained. Either George White had been murdered by Frank Fry or by a total stranger. The establishment of the military camp at nearby Bordon had resulted in 'a large influx of rough men into the district' and this, combined with evidence from a Home Office expert that the blood on Fry's clothing might well have been the result of a nosebleed, there was sufficient doubt surrounding the case. In his conclusion, the chairman of the magistrates announced:

> *Frank Fry. We have very carefully considered the evidence which has been given against you, and we consider that it is not sufficient to warrant us in committing you for trial. You are discharged.*

Fry's family burst into spontaneous applause and just moments later led him out of the court a free man. No one else was ever arrested for the murder.

CHAPTER 5

Guilt by Association:
The Case of Mabel Maud Bundy
1939

He noticed that beneath the dead woman's
right arm lay a bunch of carnations.

As Britain braced itself for war in the summer of 1939 Surrey became host to an ever-increasing number of service personnel, and it was inevitable that from time to time high spirits and skirmishes would spill out of the army camps to affect the surrounding communities. Mostly the trouble was minor, but on one or two occasions it became more serious and had a devastating impact on local inhabitants. A victim of one such incident was Mabel Maud Bundy, a forty-two-year-old staff maid at the *Moorlands Hotel*, Hindhead. Thomas Mitchell, a fellow worker at the hotel, discovered her body near a footpath among trees and bushes at six-twenty in the morning of Wednesday, 5 July 1939. Mitchell, a kitchen porter, was on his way to work from his staff quarters above the garage when he made his grim discovery. He noticed that beneath the dead woman's right arm lay a bunch of carnations.

When the pathologist, Dr Eric Gardner, examined the body at eight-thirty that same morning, he estimated that Mabel Bundy had been dead for at least eight hours but probably for no more than ten. Her death, then, would most likely have occurred between ten-thirty and half past midnight the previous night and police were swift to trace her movements leading up to those times.

Alice Dopson, who lived in Royal Parade, Hindhead, said that she had been with Mabel from about seven-thirty on the evening of 4 July, at the *Royal Huts Hotel* in Hindhead. The two women, later joined by Alice Dopson's husband, chatted in the public bar until about ten o'clock. During the course of the evening, three soldiers from the Second Battalion North Staffordshire Regiment came into the bar, had quite a few drinks and played a game of darts. At some point in the evening Mabel was approached by one of the three soldiers. He offered to buy her a drink, which she accepted, and the two engaged in conversation. At closing time, the soldier, very much Mabel's junior, insisted on escorting her to the *Moorlands Hotel* where she slept, and Alice and her husband watched the two leave arm in arm. They noticed the other two soldiers leave a short while later.

Mabel Bundy and the soldier were seen again at a quarter past ten by Randall Snelling, who lived at Moor Cottage, Grove Road. He saw them on the Portsmouth Road, opposite the turning to Grayshott Road. He noticed that the soldier was carrying a bunch of carnations, and that two other soldiers followed them as they walked. At ten minutes to eleven, three soldiers, who appeared to be in something of a hurry, were seen by Walter James Hack, at the corner of Tower Road and Portsmouth Road. They stopped by a seat near a holly hedge, conferred for a while, and after lighting up cigarettes, moved away. Mabel Bundy was no longer with them.

Following information provided by the witnesses, the police went to the army camp at Thursley on the morning of Wednesday, 5 July. There they set up an identification parade, and Private Stanley Ernest Boon was identified as one of the three soldiers who had been drinking in the *Royal Huts Hotel* the previous evening. It did not take long to name his drinking partners as Private Arthur John Smith and Private Joseph William Goodwin. Smith was recognised as the soldier who had escorted Mabel from the hotel.

The post-mortem revealed many bruises on the face and body of the dead woman. The bruises to the elbows and legs indicated that a struggle had taken place, but more serious than that were the bruises to her face. In the pathologist's opinion, the first injury to be inflicted was probably the one over her left eye, and whilst he felt it was unlikely that this single blow would have left her unconscious, it would certainly have dazed her, and, if she had been standing, knocked her to the floor. A stream of blood tricked from her nose, which was broken, and the whole of her face was generally smeared with blood. However, it was the injury to the chin which the pathologist felt to be the direct cause of death. The blow had been heavy and forced the facial bones upwards, resulting in damage to the brain. He thought the injuries were consistent with having been delivered by a fist and was quoted as saying that he thought it was, 'a forcible blow which could have been delivered by a strong man'.

The clothing worn by the three soldiers the previous evening was taken and sent for forensic examination at the Metropolitan Police Laboratory in Hendon, North London. The soldiers were taken to Farnham police station. It was noted that Smith had scratches on his face, but that the other two bore no noticeable marks.

All three men were questioned. Boon simply asserted that he had been out with Smith and Goodwin, but volunteered no further information. Smith described drinking first at a public house in Thursley, then at another in Hindhead, where they stayed until closing time. Smith explained the scratches on his face; by saying he had got them during training exercises that day. Goodwin confirmed that they had been drinking together, but insisted that, 'when we came out Smith went down the road with a woman, followed by Boon. I remained outside the hotel until they returned.' At this point Goodwin was regarded as a witness only. However, when making his statement in writing at Farnham police station, Goodwin said something, unfortunately unrecorded, that alerted the police to a greater level of involvement than had previously been thought. As soon as the police realised that he might be implicated in the crime, he was stopped and cautioned. When the case came before the magistrates, the counsel for the defence argued that any comment made by Goodwin at this juncture was inadmissible as evidence, since, as a possible witness, he had been urged by the police to tell the complete truth, 'as he had nothing to worry about'. This had lulled him into making an incriminating statement. The magistrates disagreed about the admissibility of the evidence but ordered that it should be read in camera.

After Goodwin had made a formal written statement to the police, the other two reconsidered their position and decided that it was in their best interests to give their version of events in written statements too. Smith evidently felt a sense of relief at this, commenting as he signed his statement, 'I am glad that I have told you all that; I wish that I had done before.'

Dr James Davidson of the Metropolitan Police Laboratory presented his findings to the court. Stains on the clothing of Boon and Smith had been identified as human blood, and scrapings from beneath the fingernails of the dead woman were from the surface of human skin.

The three soldiers were ordered to stand trial at the Old Bailey.

The thrust of the prosecution argument was that the soldiers, aged in their late twenties, were 'engaged in a common design to interfere with Miss Bundy, and that her death was a result of the commission of that crime.' As the accused gave evidence in the witness box, it became obvious that on the evening of the murder all three men were much the worse for drink. Boon admitted to having had seven or eight pints of beer at the *Royal Huts Hotel*, quite apart from drinks that they might have had earlier in the evening at Thursley. He was particularly drunk, and aggressively so, to such an extent that Goodwin felt the need to restrain him. Here the statements of the three soldiers become confused and contradictory. Smith admitted to having had intercourse with Mabel Bundy but was adamant that it had been with her consent. Boon, he said, later appeared beside them, put his hand over the woman's mouth and then struck her several times. Smith was taken aback by this; he did nothing to prevent it because, in his words, he 'was too flabbergasted; it all came so suddenly.' It then seems likely that Boon too had intercourse with her. Goodwin confirms most of Smith's testimony, apart from Smith's accusation that he, Goodwin, then 'followed Boon in a certain action'. In spite of the fact that Boon and Smith had known each other for some while, having spent time together in India, Boon placed all the blame on Smith and Smith all the blame on Boon. Boon admitted to covering up the woman's mouth but only because 'she was shaking her head and spitting.' Smith, he claimed, struck the blows. When Mabel went suddenly quiet, he interpreted this as consent for what then followed. He did not realise that she was dead, he said, until informed by the police the following day.

On balance the evidence pointed to Boon as the one who had dealt the fatal blows. Goodwin had tried to pull him away from the couple, but denied any physical involvement with the woman. He did not send for anyone to assist Mabel Bundy after the event as that would have been 'dragging him into it'. Smith denied any violence.

The jury of nine men and three women acquitted Goodwin of all charges, but found Smith and Boon guilty. It seemed likely that Boon and not Smith had killed Mabel Bundy, but in the eyes of the law both men were equally guilty of the crime of murder. As the prosecuting counsel explained:

If anyone was engaged in committing an act of felony in which violence was used and the death of another resulted, whether the death was contemplated or not, that person was guilty of murder. Anyone engaged in the felony, but who did not strike the blows, was also, in law, guilty of murder.

After the verdict had been announced to the court, the judge, Mr Justice Oliver, sentenced Smith and Boon to be hanged by the neck until dead. When the condemned men had been led away, he made a point of telling the jury that, in his opinion, the right decision had been made.

It is difficult to untangle the conflicting versions of events described by each of the three soldiers. But beyond dispute is the fact that one of them hit Mabel Bundy with sufficient force to kill her, and the other two did absolutely nothing to help her.

CHAPTER 6

A Cruel Mistress:
The Death of Jane Popejoy
1897

... angry crowds gathered outside the courts to jeer at the woman who had treated a seventeen-year-old girl with such cruelty.

The Victorian image of ideal womanhood was that of gentleness and goodness, patience and virtue. The nineteenth century is littered with conduct manuals written both to instruct young girls in the arts of modesty and purity, and to reinforce these qualities in the general behaviour of adult women. Why was it necessary, we might wonder, if these virtues came so naturally to the fairer sex anyway? The reality was that the image of virtuous perfection was shattered more often than anyone wished to acknowledge, and the worst culprit was the woman who wielded power over other women; the mistress of the house.

In her own domestic sphere the mistress ruled supreme. Her word was law within the confines of the home, and such power appears to have brought out the worst in a small but significant number of women.

When, in 1896, Emily Jane Popejoy, known to her family simply as Jane, obtained a post as domestic servant in the fashionable home of Mrs Camilla Nicholls in London, her family was delighted. The status of the household reflected on the status of its servants, and this was a large step forward for Jane. It was a grand house in Pitt Street, Kensington, and in the eyes of the hard-working but poor family from Bagshot, it marked a significant turn in the family fortunes. Jane would be expected to send some of her wages home, or at least to make some significant savings, and the incidental 'perks' of having a daughter in a wealthy house could have been beneficial to them all.

THE STRANGE DEATH OF A BAGSHOT SERVANT.

THE RESUMED INQUEST.
YESTERDAY.

The inquiry into the circumstances attending the death of Jane Popejoy, aged 17, a domestic servant, of Bagshot, was resumed at the Institute yesterday (Friday) by Mr. G. F. Roumieu, J.P., coroner for West Surrey, who was accompanied by the deputy-coroner, Surgeon-Major Wellington Lake. There was again a large crowd assembled at the railway station and at the entrance to the Institute, waiting the arrival of the girl's late mistress, against whom so much feeling was shown on the previous occasion. They were, however, disappointed if they expected to see Mrs. Nicholls, for she did not make her appearance, and was evidently not in attendance at the Court. The Court was densely packed when the inquiry was resumed.

Mr. Travers Humphrey, barrister, instructed by Messrs. Close and Co., appeared to watch the proceedings on behalf of the Amalgamated Societies for the Protection of Women and Children. Mr. Guy Stephenson, barrister, instructed by Messrs. Hare and Co., of Temple Chambers, again appeared to represent Mrs. Nicholls. The police were represented by Detective-Inspector Greet, of London, and Superintendent Hackman, of Chertsey. A large number of police had been drafted into the village to cope with any possible disturbance, and to preserve order.

Our readers may remember the chief facts already adduced in evidence. Briefly stated, they are as follows:— The girl Jane Popejoy is the daughter of a carpenter, living at Bagshot, and a little more than a year ago went as a domestic servant to Mrs. Nicholls, 14, Pitt Street, Kensington. She never went home till Christmas-eve, when she arrived in a dreadfully emaciated and evidently dying condition. She was dirty; her nose was broken; and she had a great number of bruises over her body; which she said were caused by her mistress. She died on Monday, December 27th. Evidence was given before the coroner as to her condition when she arrived home, and medical evidence was also given showing the result of the post-mortem examination.

A CAUTION.

Before proceeding with the inquiry, the Coroner said he desired to make a few preliminary remarks. On the last occasion he unfortunately had to clear the Court. He must impress upon the public that as long as they were in that Court they must not give vent to any feelings they might have. He did not wish for any of them to be turned out, but he must do his duty while he was conducting the case. He was conducting a very important inquiry, and in the interest of all, he hoped the public would assist him in conducting it in a straightforward and quiet way. With regard to those outside, he hoped they would behave in a better manner than they did on the former occasion. It was not for him to prejudice the case, but it was his duty to investigate it thoroughly to the end, and to get every bit of evidence possible. It would then be for the jury to arrive at a conclusion, but until they had done so, it was not right for the public to express any opinion at all. There was a very good principle in their law that everyone was considered innocent until he or she was proved guilty. He hoped this statement would

Headline from the Surrey Advertiser.
Surrey Advertiser

Jane was not the only servant to be employed at 14, Pitt Street. There was another young girl to share the domestic chores, in addition to the housekeeper, Mrs Harrington. It was true that Mrs Harrington was elderly, probably well into her eighties, but she cooked for the household, organised the meals according to Mrs Nicholls' instructions and kept a strict eye on the key to the larder. Mrs Nicholls was a widow and had a sixteen-year-old invalid daughter who required a lot of care and attention. An important part of the servants' duties was to help with the care of this daughter; she was unable to look after herself and had to be washed, dressed and taken for walks each day in a special invalid chair.

This was not Jane's first appointment though. She had been in service for at least twelve months before she went to Kensington, and this means that she may have been younger than fifteen when she first began her work as a servant; she had only just celebrated her sixteenth

Sam Milner

birthday when she went into the employment of Mrs Nicholls. Her wages in Kensington had been negotiated by her mother, Rose. She was to receive 1s 6d a week at the beginning of her employment, with the promise that this would soon be increased to 2s a week. For the daughter of a carpenter and a mother who could not read, she had done well for herself.

Jane did not see her family at all for well over a year. She began her employment in October 1896, and returned to Bagshot for the first time in December 1897. But she wrote home regularly once a month telling the family all about her life in service, how well her mistress treated her, describing all her various duties, how well they ate and even, on one occasion, how they all went to the seaside at Southsea. And she was happy to tell them that her wages had increased to 2s at the end of the first month, and then to 2s 6d not long after. Her parents were delighted and her father wrote back advising her to be good and learn all she could 'as it is the only chance you will have'.

As Christmas 1897 approached, the Popejoy family accepted the fact that they would be celebrating without Jane for the second year running. They felt sure she would be well enough where she was, but on 23 December they received a letter from Mrs Nicholls informing them that Jane was unwell and should return home as soon as possible. She was coughing so much, explained Mrs Nicholls, that despite Jane's protestations she had insisted on sending for a doctor at her own expense. The letter continued:

I was shocked and distressed beyond measure to learn from him that she must always have been consumptive... You must, the doctor says, fetch her home at once and see what native air will do; it is the only possible chance for her. Poor, poor Janey. I am too distressed even to use a pen, and it will make our Christmas very sorrowful. I cannot leave my helpless child, or I would, unwell as I am myself, have taken her.

The Popejoys were stunned. Jane had been in perfect health when they had last seen her, and this news came as a dreadful shock. They arranged for Emily, their daughter-in-law, to go to Kensington to bring Jane home the following day, but when she arrived at Pitt Street on 24 December Jane had already left; so anxious was Mrs Nicholls to get Jane out of her house that she had arranged for her to be escorted back to Bagshot by a member of the Travellers' Aid Society. She had sent her off with a parcel containing oranges, mince pies and sandwiches, but by this time Jane was too weak to eat very much at all.

When Jane finally arrived home the family barely recognised her. She was alarmingly thin, very pale and had great difficulty even standing. Her mother and sister-in-law, Ada, helped to undress her and put her to bed, and as they did they noticed that she was covered in bruises, especially on her arms and legs and even on her throat. Her clothes were filthy, as was her hair, and as they tried to clean her up Jane cried out in pain. There were running sores on two of her toes and part of a tooth was missing. Jane had always been scrupulously clean and neat in her appearance, and the women asked how she came to be in such a deplorable state. 'My mistress did it all,' Jane told them.

They brought her some food and tea but she could only manage to eat a little. She stayed in bed all the following day, and the doctor was called, but as it was Christmas Day he did not manage to see Jane until Boxing Day. By that time she was even weaker. Dr Osburn said that he 'found her extremely emaciated', with many bruises, sores and abrasions, the bridge of her nose was broken and her temperature was high. He diagnosed bronchial pneumonia, but at that point felt that she had a good chance of survival. He returned at five o'clock the following afternoon to find that her condition had deteriorated. Her pulse was now very weak and although she remained lucid she found it a great effort to talk. Nevertheless, the doctor felt compelled to ask her about her injuries.

'How did you hurt yourself?'

'Mistress.'

'How did she do it?'

'Stick,' was all she could say.

Jane died at eight o'clock that evening. She weighed just sixty-five pounds.

Three days later Police Constable Albert Yeo called at 14, Pitt Street, Kensington and asked to speak with Mrs Nicholls regarding a young girl named Jane Popejoy. 'I do not want to know anything at all about it,' she said. 'The girl is dead and I do not want to hear anything more about it.' But the choice was no longer hers; she received a summons to attend the inquest and the process to discover the truth about Jane's death had begun.

Over the course of the inquest, the magistrates' hearing and the Old Bailey trial the full story of abuse and cruelty was revealed. Mrs Camilla Nicholls had a history of abusive treatment of her servants. Jessie McNiel had been employed at 14, Pitt Street for three and a half years, and she gave evidence before the Coroner. She had frequently been beaten, she said; Mrs Nicholls would strike her or throw things at her, and two or three times she received cuts to the head, and on one occasion a black eye. If she did some thing to upset Mrs Nicholls she might be deprived of food for two or three days. 'Mrs Nicholls had a very horrid temper,' she said. 'She used to fly into a passion.' On one occasion Mrs Nicholls bolted the front door and beat her with a stick and in desperation Jessie climbed out of a window and ran away.

Elizabeth Jannaway, her successor, stayed only a month before running away. 'I left because I did not get enough food. … she pushed me across the room because I left some smears on the looking glass … she buckled me … she told me I was deceitful and discontented.' Jane's term of employment began during the short time that Elizabeth was in service and she was able to testify that Jane had been healthy, clean and strong when she arrived.

Bread and dripping seems to have formed the basis of their diet and Elizabeth encouraged Jane to write home saying that she did not like bread and dripping. When, in turn, the Popejoys wrote to Kensington about this, Mrs Nicholls was furious. She shouted at both girls, threatening to flog Elizabeth for prompting Jane to complain, and forced Jane to send another letter dictated word for word by her. It read:

Dear Mother,
I hope you will forgive me for writing all about the bread and dripping, as it is all false. I have bacon for breakfast, and the others have bread and dripping. I have a nice place and a kind mistress. I go out in the garden with the invalid.

From that day on Mrs Nicholls dictated all the letters Jane wrote home and both servants were forbidden to send even a short note without their mistress's knowledge and approval. The Popejoys, then, had no way of knowing the true nature of their daughter's situation.

Edith Garret replaced Elizabeth Jannaway after the latter found the courage to run away. Edith was made of tougher stuff than her predecessors, and played Mrs Nicholls' game by telling tales on Jane. But Edith saw everything that was going on, and was not afraid to tell the courts in spite of Mrs Nicholls' attempts to bully her into lying to the authorities. 'Jane Popejoy did not always get the whole of the meals – it was Mrs Nicholls's orders to the housekeeper that she was not to have them.' And towards the end of her time there Jane was made to take her meals in Mrs Nicholls' own private room so that no one was able to say how little or how much she was given.

Edith also witnessed the violence:

Mrs Nicholls would pull her into her room and begin fighting her with a stick – she would hit her across the back, and arms, and legs with the stick – I have seen her do it – it was a walking stick – it was kept for beating, not for walking. ... Jane had some scratches on her face, a broken nose, and a black eye. ...Her nose was broken by Mrs Nicholls with a stick in her bedroom.

On another occasion Edith says she intervened because she felt that Jane was in serious danger:

I intervened once and prevented Jane from being seriously hurt by Mrs Nicholls - she might have been killed if I had not – I saw Mrs Nicholls come at Jane with a red-hot poker – I got in front of her and Mrs Nicholls put the poker down.

She also explained how Jane's toes had been injured. Mrs Nicholls had wanted to hang a picture in one of the upstairs rooms and asked Jane to put a nail in the wall. Jane put it too high and in a fit of temper Mrs Nicholls snatched the hammer out of her hand and hit her on the foot with it. The injury remained untreated and unwashed and developed into running sores. From that moment on Jane walked with a limp.

But Camilla Nicholls had alternative explanations for all Jane's ailments, and her version of events usually involved some type of misconduct on Jane's part. Despite the evidence of numerous witnesses to the contrary, Mrs Nicholls insisted that Jane had been alarmingly thin when she began her employment. She wrote to the Popejoys to say that she had always had the greatest difficulty persuading Jane to wash her body, her hair or her clothing, and that the girl had even been reluctant to comb and brush her hair. She said the reason Jane had caught a cold five weeks before her death was that she had 'left off her drawers, and a week later she accentuated it by another most foolish act.' She did not specify what this 'foolish act' was but the blame was conveniently shifted in Jane's direction.

She told the Popejoys that Jane had a voracious appetite which, of course, she constantly indulged, but that Jane suffered from a medical condition that prevented her body from assimilating any nutrients. She ate more than anyone else in the house, sometimes five meals a day, she said, but the large amount of food did her more harm than good. To others she spun a different tale. Annie Rodd, who kept a stationer's shop in Kensington, commented to Mrs Nicholls that her servant was looking very pale and thin and that she would be ashamed to have a servant who looked so bad. Mrs Nicholls blamed the Popejoys. She said Jane had recently been home for a holiday and that her family had starved and ill-treated her. But the neighbours who saw Jane pick up dirty crusts in the street because she was so hungry, suspected otherwise.

Her cuts and bruises were purely the result of falling down, she said, often when Jane had been drinking alcohol. But the servants in the house were not the only ones to witness Camilla Nicholls' violent temper. George Taylor worked as a page next door at 16, Pitt Street, and he witnessed violence on two occasions. In October 1897 he saw Mrs Nicholls beat Janie, as he called her, on the back with an umbrella. She did this because Jane was too weak to push the invalid chair up the kerb from the road to the pavement and this angered her. One month later he saw Camilla Nicholls pull Jane inside the house by her ears and beat her across the front of her body and in the face with a stick. Jane started screaming but the door was slammed shut so he saw no more.

William Smallbones delivered milk to Pitt Street and he recalled an incident that occurred a little over a month before Jane's death. Her saw Mrs Nicholls pull one of her servants by the hair from the garden towards the front door of the house. He did not know the girl's name but she was screaming, and Mrs Nicholls responded by beating her with a stick. He called out for Mrs Nicholls to leave the girl alone to which she replied, 'Mind your own business, or else I will call a policeman.' She was confident that her superior status would override the word of a mere milkman.

However, any claim to social superiority was shattered by the end of the trial at the Old Bailey. Mrs Catherine Harrington, the housekeeper, was called to give evidence, and the court was

14, Pitt Street, Kensington. Sam Milner

stunned by her revelations. She was not just the housekeeper, she said, but Camilla Nicholls was in fact her own illegitimate daughter. She had worked as housekeeper for fifteen years after Mr Nicholls abandoned his wife and daughter: Mrs Nicholls was not, then, the widow she pretended to be. Although her husband returned when the news of her arrest for the murder of a servant hit the headlines, she had not seen him for many years before that. Her circumstances had been undeniably difficult. She was left to raise their invalid daughter on her own and with no financial support, until an elderly lady left her a small trust fund in her will. This yielded about £60 a year, but given that the rent on 14, Pitt Street was £55, this still left Mrs Nicholls with a ridiculously small income. But rather than altering her lifestyle she clung to the pretension of respectable gentility, preferring to rely on the charity of friends than to lower her social status. She could not afford one servant, much less two, and Jane in fact received no wages in all her time in Kensington.

We can only imagine why Jane tolerated her situation rather than running away as her two predecessors had done. Perhaps she did not want to let her family down; perhaps she was genuinely afraid that if she tried to run away and failed Mrs Nicholls would punish her even more severely. If she received no wages then she would have found it difficult to reach her home in Bagshot anyway.

The charge of murder was reduced to manslaughter. At every stage of the judicial process angry crowds gathered outside the courts to jeer at the woman who had treated a seventeen-year-old girl with such cruelty. Despite her confidence that her word would be believed over that of servants, Camilla Nicholls was found guilty and sentenced to seven years' penal servitude.

CHAPTER 7

The Booking Clerk Murder: Geoffrey 'Dixie' Dean
1952

... bleeding from more than twenty different stab wounds.

Today Ash Vale railway station, just six miles east of Guildford, is as unremarkable as the suburban semi-detached houses that surround it. In off-peak hours the only indication that a train will ever arrive is the hand-written note pinned to the window of the ticket office, directing would-be passengers to the self-service ticket machine at the side. But back in the 1950s it was a thriving village station, catering not only for local passengers but for

Ash Vale Railway Station. Surrey Police Archives, Mount Browne

the many troops still stationed in the district. From six in the morning till eight at night the station was manned by at least two porters and a booking clerk. The three storeys of the station building clung to the side of a steep bank, with steps leading from the entrance hall at street level to the booking office and bicycle store on the second floor, and then up to the waiting room and platforms on the third. Little would travellers have guessed, as they purchased their tickets on Friday, 22 August 1952, that the young booking clerk handing them their change would take his last breath that very evening beneath the spindly legs of the stool on which he sat, bleeding from more than twenty different knife wounds.

James John Alcott held the dubious distinction of being one of the few people to have heard himself sentenced to death twice, for two separate and brutal murders, committed years apart. The first was of a night watchman, murdered in Germany in 1948 whilst Alcott was serving with the Grenadier Guards. The evidence clearly pointed to Alcott as the killer, and at the court martial he was found guilty and sentenced to death. For reasons that are hard to fathom, this first death sentence was not confirmed, a bewildering omission that held the most devastating consequences for the twenty-seven-year-old booking clerk, Geoffrey Charles Dean, who died four years later at the hands of Alcott, leaving a five-year-old daughter and a wife who was carrying a second baby, due early the following year.

There had never been any doubt that Alcott was destined for trouble, even from his early years. Having been caught by the police at the age of eleven for stealing a bicycle, and again a year later for stealing money, he was sent to the National Children's Home for three years. It was during this time that he came to know the area around Ash Vale. After serving a prison sentence for stealing another bicycle, he enlisted and set out on the path to his first killing.

By 1952 Alcott, having survived one death sentence, was still only twenty-three-years-old. He was living with his wife in her grandmother's flat in Eltham and working as a railway fireman at the Hither Green depot. He was a large, fair-haired young man, six feet tall and very muscular, and his wife found nothing in his behaviour to alert her to his darker side. From her point of view theirs was a happy marriage, marred only slightly by an occasional shortage of funds, but this was hardly unusual for a young couple. They had planned to spend their annual vacation in France, at the home of Alcott's French mother-in-law, and on the first day of the holiday, 18 August 1952, Alcott left his wife at home while he went to collect the £16 he had saved for his holiday. He told his wife he was going to get a haircut, but in fact the first thing he did was to buy a knife in a brown leather sheath, at a cost of fifteen shillings; he clearly felt there was one more job he needed to do before crossing the Channel.

Alcott's planning was careful. He spent a great deal of time in and around Ash Vale Station over the next few days. A junior booking clerk named Jones remembered him asking about the times of boat trains between Victoria and Dover on Wednesday, 20 August. He was recognised again the following day by a senior clerk, Norman Thompson, when he asked to use the telephone in the office. Alcott used his British Rail staff pass to gain admittance, and gave a story about needing to check on the progress of a colleague who had been injured in an accident. He got no reply and used this as an excuse to loiter around the booking office. He was waiting for a return call, he said, and was anxious about the state of his workmate as he had inadvertently caused the accident himself whilst removing coals from his fire. Alcott clearly felt relaxed and confident that his story was believed, as he was found by a porter in the staff room later that day cleaning his nails with his knife.

He returned to the station in the evening, chatting to the porters about his work, his wife and his injured colleague. At the end of the evening Norman Thompson offered him a lift home on the back of his motorcycle. This meant that Alcott was around to observe the cashing up and locking up procedures in the office.

On the day of the murder, Friday, 22 August, Alcott was noticed by one of the porters, Harrington, during the early part of the evening. He once more asked permission to use the booking office telephone. At twenty to eight, when a signalman went into the office to use the telephone himself, he found Alcott and Dean talking amicably together. Dean even left Alcott alone in the booking office for a short time while he took tickets and date stamps to Harrington.

At about a quarter to eight a passenger, Corporal K G Vincent, approached the booking office window to purchase a ticket, but the wooden shutter had been pulled down. He knocked several times on the counter but received no reply. He heard some noises inside, scuffling noises and voices, but nothing disturbing enough to alert him to what was happening, or about to happen behind the locked door. A notice advising passengers to purchase tickets from the porter after eight o'clock was propped against the window, so Corporal Vincent left in search of a ticket. Fifteen minutes later Cedric Bull, a station porter, looked through a window into the booking office and saw Dean's legs and feet on the floor, splattered with blood. Blood also stained the wooden floor around him, and the door to the office safe was open. In alarm he called Hill, a fellow porter, and together they broke down the door to the booking office. Dean was dead and £168 was missing from the safe.

Booking Office where Geoffrey Dean was killed. Surrey Police Archives, Mount Browne

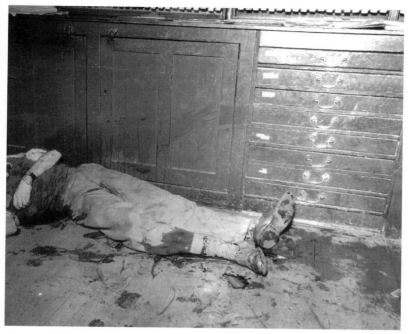

Body of Geoffrey Dean. Surrey Police Archives, Mount Browne

The police were prompt to take control of the scene of the crime. First to arrive was PC Shinar, closely followed by Sergeant D Forehead, a local officer who knew Dean personally. Various items were found on the floor of the booking office, including keys, a cigarette lighter and the broken dentures from Dean's mouth. The body was taken to Farnham Mortuary for the post-mortem; it revealed the cause of death to be haemorrhage from twenty stab wounds.

The following day, the officer in charge of the investigation, Superintendent Tom Roberts, initiated a search of local hostels and boarding houses and enquiries were made about any suspicious guests. Following information given by Mrs Dagger of 10, Victoria Road, Aldershot, the police searched a bedroom on her premises and found a bloodstained jacket. Several days later a police dog found the matching blue trousers wrapped in brown paper beneath some gorse bushes on a nearby common. Witnesses at the station described Alcott as having worn a navy blue suit and white shirt on the evening of the murder. The jacket and trousers matched this description. When Alcott, who had taken the room in Victoria Road, returned at a quarter past eleven that night he was searched by police who found £109 10s in banknotes. Alcott volunteered the information that the knife was hidden in the chimney. He had taken his shoes, which were also bloodstained, to a cobbler for repair, but not before replacing them with new ones.

It seemed as though Alcott was expecting the police to find him. He offered no resistance and when cautioned confessed:

I have been down there three days. I hung about for a long time and then went in. We had quite a struggle and I left my fingerprints on the desk. I was going to France on holiday. I didn't really want money. I had my own.

Alcott claimed that he had been deeply disturbed by the injury to his colleague, and that this had prompted him to kill Dean. In his words:

I took out my knife from my pocket and attacked Dean by stabbing him. He struggled and kicked at me, shouting to Paddy, the porter, but I just stabbed him one after the other. I took what money there was in the booking office and put it in my pocket.

At Alcott's trial at the Surrey Assizes in November 1952, no witnesses were called for the defence. His counsel, Mr du Cann, put it to the jury that Alcott was suffering from a bout of temporary insanity at the time of the crime. He was not suggesting, he went on to explain, that Alcott was insane at the time of his trial, but that at the time of the murder, 'he was momentarily under a defect of reason due to a diseased mind, which caused him not to appreciate the nature and quality of his act.' Alcott's behaviour confirmed this theory, he argued. His visits to the station were frequent and overt, he registered at the boarding house in his own name, he could easily have used his passport and tickets to travel to France following the murder, he failed to dispose of all the bloodstained clothing, and if theft had been his motive he could have taken the money during the short time that Dean left him alone in the booking office. 'If he was trying to assist justice he could hardly have done more,' concluded Mr du Cann. The judge did not appear to be of the same opinion. Mr Justice Finnemore, in his summing up, told the jury:

> *There is no evidence that he suffered from any disease of the mind and did not know quite well what he was doing and did not know that it was wrong. ... There is no evidence in this case in which you can reasonably come to the conclusion that this man was insane when he committed the crime. You may think it is extremely difficult to see what other defence there might have been.*

The jury of ten men and two women took little more than twenty minutes to reach their verdict of 'guilty', and as the death sentence was passed Alcott stood to soldierly attention. When asked whether he wished to say anything, he replied, 'Nothing whatsoever, Your Honour'.

An appeal was heard on Wednesday, 17 December 1952 by Lord Chief Justice, Lord Goddard, Mr Justice Hallet and Mr Justice Hilbery. The appeal was lodged on the grounds that in the original trial Mr Justice Finnemore had been wrong to direct the jury not to consider the verdict of 'guilty but insane'. But the appeal judges supported the original decision, stating openly that the argument for appeal was totally hopeless and reaffirming that, 'There was not a shred of evidence he was suffering from any defect of reason.'

James John Alcott was hanged at Wandsworth prison. Following custom, a post-mortem was carried out immediately, much to the discomfort of the officer in attendance, Superintendent Roberts, who reported that a post-mortem on such a recently deceased body was, 'a very different experience'.

On Friday, 5 September 1952 British Rail colleagues, local villagers and family members gathered at the medieval church of St Peter at Ash to pay their last respects to Geoffrey Dean, known to his workmates as Dixie. As the cortège approached

Church of St Peter at Ash. Sam Milner

the church, villagers carrying sprays of flowers joined with railway workers to line its route to the church door. Later, at the cemetery, as the coffin was lowered into its grave, a train

on the nearby railway line slowed down on its approach to Ash Vale Station, a last mark of respect for the young booking clerk who lost his life so needlessly.

Gravestone of Geoffrey Dean. Sam Milner

CHAPTER 8

Fight or Flight: The Shooting of the Vicar of Frimley
1850

The Reverend Hollest went to his dressing room to fetch the handgun he always kept loaded there, and he pursued the burglars ...

f you wake in the night to find burglars in your home then a difficult decision has to be made. Do you put yourself at risk and make a stand or do you simply acquiesce to the intruders' demands? This was the dilemma facing the vicar of Frimley, the Reverend George Hollest, and his wife Caroline on the night of 27 September 1850. At three o'clock in the morning the couple were woken in the night. In Mrs Hollest's words, 'I noticed an increase of light in the room, but could not perceive how it was occasioned.' Although the curtains around the bed were open at the foot end, they obscured the view of the rest of the room. At first the Reverend Hollest sought to reassure his wife, telling her not to be afraid, that it was only their two sons who had returned that day from school, playing a prank. Mrs Hollest did not for one moment believe this to be the case, and reached out through the curtains to ring the bell for the servants. She was stopped, however, and grabbed by a man wearing a mask. As she tried to scream out another man took hold of the Reverend Hollest, and the couple were warned by the armed men to be silent or they would have their brains blown out. The vicar and his wife were of they same mind: they each decided not to give in to the burglars but to continue to struggle.

Mrs Hollest was forced to the floor in the narrow space between the bed and the wall. She could not see her attacker but was struck by the unusual quality of his voice; it had a strangely squeaky tone. It was then that she heard a pistol being fired on her husband's side of the bed. With a renewed sense of urgency she struggled to reach her husband, with her assailant still holding her around the waist and still pressing the pistol into her side. She saw that her husband was now struggling with two men. Fortunately, her attacker caught his foot on the washstand and almost pulled it over. This gave Mrs Hollest the opportunity she needed to reach out for the hand bell sitting on the fender, and she managed to raise the alarm.

The intruders now tried to flee. The Reverend Hollest went to his dressing room to fetch the handgun he always kept loaded there, and he pursued the burglars out of the front door of the house into the front garden. Mrs Hollest watched from an open window as the three men ran outside to join a fourth who had been waiting beneath a tree. As one of them turned to look directly at her she took fright and slammed the window shut.

A few minutes later the Reverend Hollest returned to join his wife. Calmly he informed her, 'The fellow has shot me.' Mrs Hollest now saw that her husband was bleeding from the stomach, and she immediately sent their servant, Giles, to fetch both the local surgeon and the constable. Making sure to lock the staircase door for fear that one of the burglars might return, she bound her husband's wound as well as she could and tried to stem the flow of blood. The injury must have been the result of the shot fired in the bedroom, but so intent was the vicar on protecting his household from the intruders that he had not realised he had been shot.

When the surgeon, Dr Davis, arrived he found the Reverend Hollest in bed but in good spirits and certainly not expecting to die. On examining him he found a gunshot wound about one inch below the navel and realised that the injury was very serious indeed. He stayed with his patient and tended him throughout the night. The Reverend Hollest died at one o'clock the following day. Dr Davis himself carried out the post mortem and discovered a marble lodged in the vicar's abdomen. He had no doubt whatsoever that this injury had been the direct cause of George Hollest's death.

Four men were arrested as a result of persistent detective work, helped no doubt by the offer of a £150 reward for information leading to the capture of the culprits, a reward for which the police were also eligible at this time. The men were Levi Harwood and Samuel Harwood, brothers of twenty-nine and twenty-five years of age respectively, twenty-four-year-old James Jones and Richard Fowler, age unknown, who generally went by the name of Hiram Smith. The investigation was aided considerably by the fact that Smith decided to turn Queen's evidence and tell the police everything he knew, in the hope that he would both escape punishment and receive at least some of the reward. The full story of the burglary then came to light.

Hiram Smith and James Jones were both lodged at the *Wheatsheaf* public house in Guildford. Levi Harwood was staying at the Swan beer shop, also in Guildford. Smith was a particular friend of Samuel Harwood and the two had planned to go to a prize fight in Frimley. Jones, who appears to have been the mastermind behind the crime, asked the pair to call in at Grove House, the vicarage where the Hollest family lived, on their way to the fight. His plan was that under the pretext of selling dishes door to door, Smith and Harwood could check out the premises and pick up any information that might be of use to them in carrying out the burglary. Eleanor Vanner, the housemaid in the vicarage, recalled their visit. She bought none of the dishes, and when they asked her for some food, refused them, denying them entry to the house. She remembered that they seemed rather angry about this.

Jones then laid his plans for the burglary. He asked Hiram Smith to join the group that Friday night, and although the latter initially refused, when he heard that the others were prepared to take part in Jones' plan, he too agreed to go. Frimley is about ten miles from Guildford, and the four accomplices made their way independently, meeting at a prearranged location on the edge of a common two miles from their destination. The Harwood brothers brought the pistols, and Smith watched Levi load each one with a stony marble. Jones carried one pistol in his pocket and Levi Harwood took the other. Each of the men was given a mask.

The point of entry into the house was a small scullery window. As the smallest of the party Smith forced his way between the bars, and from the inside drilled out the central bar so that Levi Harwood and James Jones could follow him. Samuel Harwood remained outside, waiting beneath a cypress tree in the garden. The three then searched the house for plunder, taking food from the pantry, a gold watch, several silver items, coins, clothing and anything else they felt would fetch a reasonable price. Together they drank some wine kept in a box by the passage, and not even Samuel was forgotten. Smith filled a decanter with wine and took it outside to his friend, even thinking to steal an umbrella for him because by this time it was raining. Having helped themselves to articles from the rest of the house, they went upstairs to the Hollests' bedroom. According to Smith it was Levi Harwood who fired the pistol into George Hollest, and James Jones who attacked Caroline. This detail was contradicted by Caroline Hollests' evidence; when confronted by the prisoners in police custody, she recognised Levi Harwood's distinctively squeaky voice as that of her own assailant.

As the men made their escape they dropped much of the booty, but managed to hold on to the bag of coins. This later proved unfortunate for them, as the coins formed the major part of a collection of subscriptions for the Frimley National Schools Association, and included some easily identifiable tokens collected by the local schoolteacher, Caroline Bullpen. The tokens were tangible evidence that the men had indeed been the Frimley vicarage burglars.

Inspector Charles Hollington of the Guildford police took James Jones and Levi Harwood into custody on the Sunday after the burglary. His colleague, Inspector Kendall, had already noted some bloodstained footprints on the doorstep of the vicarage. As the police searched the prisoners' premises they found a bloodstained stocking in Levi Harwood's lodgings, and on examination noticed that his right foot had several small cuts. Smith confirmed that the three of them had removed their shoes before breaking into the vicarage.

Levi's brother Samuel was arrested the following day, Monday, 30 September. Louisa Hollington, the wife of Inspector Charles Hollington, was at Guildford police station on 2 October, while the Harwood brothers were being held in custody, and she overheard a conversation between them. In fairness to them she had already warned them that 'a still tongue makes a wise head', but the need to communicate with each other overrode their caution. She recalled the conversation at their trial.

'Tidler,' Levi was supposed to have called out.

'Halloa,' Samuel replied, 'who is that?'

'Me.'

'Is it Bona?' asked Samuel.

'Yes.'

'Come here.'

'I can't. I'm locked up,' Levi told him. The two then tried to find out from each other how far the police had got in their investigation, until Levi remembered that they might be overheard, and called out, 'Tidler put your mouth down and don't speak so loud or else Mrs Hollington will hear you.' Then he ended with this instruction, 'Mind, you and I have not had half a pint of beer together for three or four months.'

But any attempt to claim that they had not seen each other for months was fruitless. The evidence weighed heavily against them. James Jones and the Harwood brothers were brought to trial at the April Assizes 1851. Their counsel put up a spirited defence, pouring scorn on the evidence of Hiram Smith and even suggesting that Smith was in fact the murderer. Samuel Harwood, counsel argued, had not even been present in the house. This last line of argument was successful as Samuel Harwood was found not guilty. But, although the foreman declared that the entire jury was convinced that neither Levi nor Jones had actually pulled the trigger, the two were nevertheless found guilty and sentenced to death. In his address to the prisoners the judge, Mr Baron Parke, explained why the law required him to pass such a sentence on them. To attack an innocent man in the middle of the night and in his own home was an extremely serious crime. Furthermore he was reported to have said:

Although it was possible that the death of the deceased was not the result of an act committed by either of them, and that it was not their hand that fired the fatal shot, yet they were legally and properly convicted of the crime of wilful murder, and that he trusted their fate would be a warning to others.

Three Villains Hanging. Surrey Advertiser and Surrey Times

The fate of Hiram Smith at this point remained uncertain. He was being held in custody for an unconnected burglary in the home of Mrs Harriet Stoner in Sussex. But this was not the crime that was uppermost in his mind; the extent of his role in the Hollest murder, as revealed at the trial of Jones and Harwood, weighed far more heavily on him. He was by no means off the hook. Unless one or other of his accomplices confessed to actually firing the shot that killed George Hollest, he might still find himself facing the gallows. As his former friends awaited their execution at Horsemonger Lane Gaol, Smith was being held in a different part of the same prison, anxiously awaiting news.

On Friday, 4 April 1851 Mr Sparkes, the High Sheriff, and Mr Smallpiece, the Under Sheriff, delivered the execution warrants for James Jones and Levi Harwood. The *Daily News* reported that:

[the prisoners] *were told that no hope could be entertained of their lives being saved. Jones received the announcement in a deplorable state, but Harwood seemed rather indifferent.*

They had eleven days in which to contemplate their execution. And it was not only Harwood and Jones who suffered during this time; Hiram Smith became more agitated with every passing day, praying that one of the two would confess before

Old Guildford Road, Frimley. Sam Milner

their deaths, or else he knew he might well be joining them. On Wednesday, 16 April, the day after the hanging, Smith was informed that Levi Harwood had finally confessed to firing the shot that killed George Hollest. Whether Harwood really was the murderer or whether he was merely trying to save his old friend will never be known, but Smith's relief must have been immense. He was so relieved, in fact, that it took him only a few moments to recover sufficiently to express his hope that he would now be given some of the £150 reward. No records survive to tell us whether or not he received any money, but many would feel that he was fortunate enough to have escaped with his life.

CHAPTER 9

Mercy Killing: The Death of Helena Storey
1958

'I have just shot my mother.'

Although it is virtually impossible ever to condone the act of murder, on very rare occasions it is possible to feel a certain degree of sympathy for all parties involved in the case, even for the perpetrator of the crime. Such is the case of nineteen-year-old Alec Taylor Lawrence and the murder of his foster mother Helena Emily Storey, in February 1958.

To all appearances the Storeys were model residents of Pirbright Green, living thoroughly respectable lives in their 400-year-old converted farmhouse. George Storey was an accountant and travelled daily to his offices in London.

Headline from The Daily Mirror *showing artist's impression of Alec Lawrence.*
Daily Mirror

The 'CINDERELLA' MIND OF A BOY KILLER . . .

ALEC LAWRENCE
He shot foster-mother

A "CINDERELLA" complex—a feeling that he did not belong to anybody—helped to drive Alec Taylor Lawrence, 19, to kill his wealthy foster-mother in their village home, it was said yesterday.

It was also said that Lawrence—the lad from a bombed-out home who was sent by his foster-parents to a public school—had a "sense of failure."

Lawrence, a National Service soldier, was accused at the Old Bailey of the capital murder of his foster-mother, Mrs. Helena Emily Storey, 52, in a 400-year-old converted farmhouse at Pirbright Green, Surrey. And it was his counsel, Mr. F. H. Lawton, Q.C., who compared him with Cinderella.

The court was told that Lawrence—on leave from the Army—called at the village police station and said he had shot his foster-mother with an automatic pistol, which he produced.

Then Mr. Lawton told the "Cinderella" story of Alec Lawrence. It was a story in two parts.

PART ONE: In North London in 1940 Lawrence—then aged two—was dug out of the debris of his bombed home.

The 'fairy godmother' Mrs. Storey and her husband, who were neighbours, took the boy in, said Mr. Lawton. Mr. Storey

'Felt he did not belong'

psychiatrist who examined him told the court.

Lawrence thought his foster mother was going blind—and had the idea of "putting her out of her misery."

Lawrence was found not guilty of capital murder but guilty of

Helena was actively involved in local affairs and charities; she was the local organiser of the National Savings Movement, and was deeply immersed in charity work, especially for the elderly. Alec was known to friends and neighbours as Alec Storey; no one had the least idea that he was not their natural son. He was expensively educated at Mill Hill and treated by the Storeys entirely as if he were their own.

But Alec was, as events later proved, a deeply disturbed young man and his history was far from straightforward. He was born in the early years of the Second World War to the Lawrence family who lived in North London. At that time the Storeys also lived in North London and were neighbours to the Lawrences. When Alec was two years old the family home was bombed. Later newspaper reports claimed that Alec had to be dug out from the débris of his former home. The Lawrences were not wealthy and struggled to re-house their family. It was at this point that Helena and George Storey offered to help by taking in little Alec. The Lawrences refused to consider adoption, but readily acknowledged that the Storeys could give Alec the sort of life that they simply could not afford. He spent more and more time with the Storeys, and when they eventually moved to Pirbright he moved with them. He never lost touch with his natural family, though. However, as the years passed, far from becoming more settled in his situation, Alec's feelings of displacement grew. It can be hard for a young child to understand that he is living with a foster family purely for his own good, however well he is treated. His brothers and sisters remained with his natural parents and the fact that he was not living with them opened up an emotional gap. This gap was widened as Alec's education distanced him further from his siblings. He felt guilt and confusion as his speech became different and his experiences at public school stood out in marked contrast to theirs.

On the other side of the equation, Alec had a distinct sense of letting his foster family down. He did not do particularly well at school, failing in three subjects in his General School Certificate in 1954. This was a huge source of stress to Alec. In the run up to the exams he lost weight and was prone to bouts of vomiting. His doctor described him as 'suffering from an anxiety state.' At his trial a psychiatrist, Dr Walter Neustater, stated that in his opinion:

> *Lawrence was suffering from marked hysteria, which was an abnormality of the mind. He needed psychological as well as physical treatment, as here was some immaturity which might respond to glandular treatment.*

At the Old Bailey trial, Alec Lawrence's defence counsel, Mr F H Lawton QC, compared his state of mind to that of Cinderella; 'he did not belong to anybody, either to Mr and Mrs Storey or to his parents,' he said.

Close up of the artist's impression of Alec Lawrence. Daily Mirror

At the time of the murder Lawrence was at home with the Storeys, on leave from the Army in which he was doing his National Service. On the day in

Pirbright Green, home of the Storey family. Sam Milner

question, 11 February 1958, Alec borrowed a .22 automatic pistol and seventeen rounds of ammunition from a neighbour. He said he needed to do some target practice, presumably in the garden of his home. But Alec took the pistol to his bedroom and shot a round into the floor. He said this was accidental. Helena Storey was obviously alarmed at hearing a shot in the house but Alec came downstairs to apologise to his foster mother, and together they went upstairs to inspect the damage to the carpet. Alec was still carrying the pistol. Helena Storey was clearly upset by what had happened and sat down in a chair by the mirror in Alec's room. In his statement to the police he explained:

> *She then got down on the floor to look at the bullet hole. While she was like that I pulled the trigger which resulted in her being hit in the head. I think she jerked forward straight away and fell flat on her tummy, with her head on its left side. I then aimed a second shot at her and emptied the magazine at her head.*

Alec was convinced that Helena had been killed by the first shot, but decided to shoot again to be completely sure.

At half past two that afternoon Alec Lawrence walked into Knaphill police station and made a confession. 'I have just shot my mother,' he said. 'She is lying dead in the bedroom. I put a lot of bullets in her head.' It is worth noting that Alec referred to Helena Storey here as 'my mother'.

That Alec Lawrence's mind was in turmoil was easy to see, but this was not enough to explain why he had committed such an appalling act of violence against his foster mother. In his statement to the police he explained exactly what had prompted the killing. Here he refers to Mrs Storey as 'Lena':

> *Last Tuesday Lena told me her bad eyesight was due to her health, but they were trying to fix her up with some glasses to stop her going blind. This was a great shock to me. I felt stunned.*

In Alec Lawrence's mind, then, this was a mercy killing. He said he had often wondered what he should do if anything awful happened to her, such as becoming crippled or blind,

View across Pirbright Green. Sam Milner

and he had already decided that the kindest course of action would be to 'put her out of any misery she might be liable to suffer'. He was convinced that she was going blind, possibly without any real evidence; Helena Storey's revelation might well have contained an element of anecdotal exaggeration rather than being a literal medical diagnosis. But with his foster mother kneeling on the floor in front of him and the pistol in his hand, it was the ideal opportunity to put his resolve into practice.

Lawrence's feelings towards Helena Storey were clearly confused, but equally clearly involved a large measure of affection, gratitude and a sense of obligation. This was taken into consideration by the jury who found him not guilty of capital murder but guilty instead of manslaughter.

The judge, Mr Justice Ashworth, expressed his approval of the jury's decision, but in sentencing Lawrence to three years' imprisonment, explained that it was his duty to deal with the seriousness of the crime. He then addressed Alec Lawrence directly:

Everyone in this court trusts that the future will be rosy, but much may depend on you. I trust that at the end of it you will be able to come out and be a man.

CHAPTER 10

Regency Parricide: The Murder of George Chennell
1817

*'he became for a moment humanised,
and tears ran down his cheeks.'*

Murder not only affects those most closely concerned, the victims, their families and neighbours, but it often has an impact on the wider community. The shock reverberates throughout a neighbourhood, stirring disbelief, fear and anger. Such was the reaction of the inhabitants of Godalming following the murder of George Chennell Senior and his housekeeper, Elizabeth Wilson, on 10 November 1817. Both had been killed by repeated blows to the head, followed by deep cuts to the neck and throat. The death of seemingly quiet, respectable people was shocking in itself, but this murder aroused even greater indignation in Godalming when it was revealed that the murderers were none other than William Chalcraft, George Chennell's own employee, and worse still, his son, also called George Chennell. Parricide is a particularly ugly word.

Guildford High Street, scene of mass demonstrations against the murderers of George Chennell and Elizabeth Wilson. Surrey History Centre

MURDER! and PARRICIDE!!!

An original and authentic Report

OF THE

Trial

OF

GEORGE CHENNELL

AND

W. CHALCRAFT,

For the most horrid

MURDER,

OF

Mr. GEORGE CHENNELL, Sen.
(Father of the Prisoner G. Chennell)

AND OF

ELIZABETH WILSON,
(His House-keeper)

At Godalming,

SURREY.

WHO WERE CONVICTED AT THE

SUMMER ASSIZE, AT GUILDFORD,

BEFORE

MR. SERGEANT LENS.

On WEDNESDAY the 11th of AUGUST 1818.

Taken in Short-Hand.

PRINTED AND PUBLISHED BY S. RUSSELL AND CO.
LIBRARY, GUILDFORD,
AND SOLD BY ALL BOOKSELLERS.

By permission of the British Library

The outrage caused by this double murder was so great, that by six o'clock on the morning of the trial, Wednesday, 11 August 1818, the crowds were already gathering outside the Town Hall at Guildford to claim a place inside the courtroom. Over the next two hours the numbers swelled until the authorities were afraid that the doors would be forced open. The Officers of the Peace of Guildford were called to restore order, but even this was not enough; the Javelin men, members of the sheriff's escort who were armed with pikes, were also needed to stop the crowds from getting out of control. By eight o'clock, when the prisoners were taken to the dock, they had to walk through a pressing crowd of spectators. Even the counsel for the prosecution, Mr Gurney, warned the jury not to allow their outrage to influence their judgement; 'let not those feelings of resentment and indignation, which it is impossible to repress indeed, lead you to believe more readily that they are guilty,' he advised. Chennell seemed to be more affected by the attitude of the crowds than Chalcraft, who remained cool throughout the proceedings.

Chennell was known for his quiet ways; during his time in prison he always avoided trouble wherever possible and, unlike other inmates, was never prone to fighting. He had been ambitious though, and after his marriage to the daughter of a highly respected farmer in Chiddingfold nine years earlier, he had used the marriage settlement of £2,000 to set himself up in his own farm. He soon became accustomed to a more extravagant lifestyle; he enjoyed entertaining but when funds began to run dry he turned instead to drinking in public houses and shunning the company of his wife in favour of lower-class women. Not surprisingly his marriage failed, and at the time of the murders Chennell was living in a rented room in the lodging house of a Mrs Stillwell in Godalming, although he took most of his meals at his father's house.

It was well known that father and son were not on good terms. As for the son's relationship with Elizabeth Wilson, the other murder victim, she had worked as housekeeper for the family for thirty years, and when Chennell's mother died during his infancy she took over the maternal role. Neighbours described her attitude to him as warm and affectionate throughout his life, but it was an affection that Chennell junior did not return. On many occasions he was heard to say that he wished both his father and the housekeeper dead, especially the housekeeper, whom he regarded as nosey and interfering. These were comments that returned to haunt him at his trial.

Chalcraft was judged by the mores of the day as being 'of bad character'. He spent a great deal of time drinking in public houses and was negligent both as a husband and a father. He had long failed to properly support his wife and six children, giving them a meagre portion of his earnings and leaving them instead to be supported by the parish. His relationship with the younger Chennell was unusual for its day; strictly speaking it should have been that of master and servant as Chalcraft worked as carter to the Chennell family, but their friendship crossed the social divide and they soon became constant drinking companions.

At the opening of the trial the prosecuting counsel, Mr Gurney, outlined the events surrounding the murders to the members of the jury. The body of Elizabeth Wilson had been discovered in

House of George Chennell in Godalming High Street. By permission of the British Library

the front kitchen of the house, and that of George Chennell senior in his bed. Both had been murdered in the same way; first by hammer blows fracturing their skulls, then by having their throats slit with a knife. The surgeon's evidence suggested that the initial blows to the head had been the principal cause of death, as indicated by the relative lack of blood around the knife wounds.

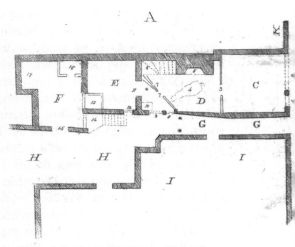

Plan of the home of George Chennell. By permission of the British Library

Both Chennell and Chalcraft vigorously denied the charge of murder and claimed they had not seen each other since the previous Friday. This gave the prosecution an opportunity to produce the first damaging evidence against the two accused. Witness after witness came forward to testify that they had seen Chennell and Chalcraft together in the passage beside George Chennell's house, shortly after nine o'clock on the Monday evening. When pressed as to their certainty of its being the accused, all but one appeared quite convinced that the figures seen in the passage were none other than Chennell and Chalcraft and another woman. Several of them mentioned the light shed by the butcher's shop window, leaving them no room for doubt.

The second line of argument put forward by the prosecution concerned the exact timing of the murders. It was important to narrow down, as far as possible, the time of the deaths. George Chennell was known to be a man of predictable habits, and he usually retired to bed at nine o'clock. A neighbour informed the court that Elizabeth Wilson intended sitting up after this time in order to work on a shirt she was sewing for Chennell junior. The two had last been seen alive at eight o'clock. Other neighbours living on the other side of the passage were able to affirm that all was quiet in the Chennell

Godalming High Street showing the Great George *public house, and the site of the* Little George. Godalming Museum, previously published by R Head 'Godalming in Old Picture Postcards'

household up to nine o'clock. Charlotte Hales, who lived next door at the *Little George Inn*, had her bedroom directly adjacent to George Chennell's on the other side of a thin partition wall. She claimed she could generally hear everything from the drawing of the curtains to Chennell coughing in bed, but on the night of the murders she heard nothing from the time she went to bed at ten to ten to the time she fell asleep after eleven. No noises woke her in the night. This made, according to the prosecution, the span between nine o'clock and ten to ten the most likely time for the murders. It also fitted with the time witnesses say they saw Chennell and Chalcraft in the passage next to the house.

Chennell admitted that he had visited his father that evening, but much earlier and only for a very short

The home of George Chennell today. The upper window marks the bedroom of George Chennell senior. Sam Milner

The passage beside the house of George Chennell, where Chennell and Chalcraft were seen by witnesses. Sam Milner

time. He did not stop to eat but took some food in his hand to eat as he left. He went to the *Richmond Arms*, a favourite public house in Godalming, where he spent most of the evening, apart from a few minutes when he left to meet a woman. He was gone for such a short time, he claimed, that the pipe he had been smoking was still alight on his return. The landlord of the *Richmond Arms*, James Tidy, gave evidence to the contrary. According to him Chennell had been drinking beer in his public house, but left at about nine o'clock. He returned at a quarter to ten, and Tidy was sure his pipe was not still alight because Chennell ordered a new pipe from him and a pennyworth of tobacco, as well as some brandy and more beer. He saw Chennell finally leave at about half past eleven. The *Richmond Arms*, then, gave Chennell nothing by way of an alibi.

The murders were discovered the following morning at seven-thirty. A handful of employees, including Chalcraft, arrived at six thirty to await orders for the day. Strangely, no one was about and speculation began as to why the usually punctual George Chennell was still in bed. By seven thirty everyone became restless and started to look around. Chalcraft called up the stairs to wake his master. This was a mistake, as another witness, George Austen, informed the court that it was impossible to call up from the foot of the stairs without seeing the body of Elizabeth Wilson lying on the floor of the front kitchen. Yet Chalcraft had not raised the alarm.

Further incriminating evidence came from the discovery of two bloodstained pound notes found in a chest in Chennell's room, and some stains, also thought to be of blood, on the labourer's frock worn by Chalcraft. But the prosecution's final coup was in producing a witness who appeared to have been an accomplice. However, both the prosecuting counsel and the judge were careful to point out to the jury that since this witness was a woman of doubtful reputation, and possibly also of 'a perturbed state of mind' her evidence should be regarded as unreliable, and only heeded when it was corroborated by the statements of other witnesses. Unreliable or not, Sarah Hurst testified that she had been asked by Chalcraft to go with him shortly after nine on the evening on Monday, 10 November, and to keep watch outside George Chennell's house, while he and Chennell junior went inside. Afterwards she was offered £4 for her services, which she refused. When she asked what they had done, Chalcraft was supposed to have replied, 'Done? We have done for them both.' Sarah Hurst's testimony was a point of high drama in the courtroom. One reporter stated that she 'was so much agitated, that at first, it was with great difficulty any answers could be obtained,' and at one point she even fainted.

It took the jury no more than three minutes to find both men guilty of the murders of George Chennell senior and Elizabeth Wilson.

The judge, Mr Sergeant Lens, then donned the black coif to pass sentence. The victims in this case had deserved the reverence and protection of the accused, and this aggravated an already loathsome crime, he said. 'No mercy can be extended here below, for such a deed as this.' And with that he sentenced them both to be hanged and their bodies dissected according to the law. Chalcraft called out, protesting his innocence; Chennell appeared unmoved.

The two were taken back to separate cells in Guildford Gaol. The following day they received a final visit from their wives and children. Chalcraft's wife brought all six of their offspring, the youngest of whom was just twelve months old, and despite all the difficulties they had endured, the whole family was in tears. His wife begged him to confess for the sake of his immortal soul, but nothing other than a declaration of his innocence was forthcoming.

Chennell, who up to this point had appeared hardened and unmoved, softened at the sight of his estranged wife and their eight-year-old child. In the words of an onlooker, 'he became for a moment humanised, and tears ran down his cheeks.' They had lived apart for nearly two years, but with the awfulness of the following day's execution overshadowing them, the two took this final opportunity to show affection and forgiveness.

At nine o'clock on the morning of Friday, 14 August 1818, the prisoners were taken from Guildford gaol to the place of execution at Godalming Meadows, accompanied by a cavalcade of officials, clergymen, gaolers and officers. Their hands were tied, and the rope with which they were to be hanged was placed behind them. Their wagon was specially designed with a stepped platform at the rear from where they would climb to the gallows. In the front of the wagon sat the executioner carrying a drawn sword. When they reached Godalming Meadows, having driven through crowds of silent onlookers, Chalcraft was still protesting his innocence, but to no avail. The *Observer* printed a report of the manner of their deaths on 16 August. It read:

[Chennell] *stood firm and upright without the least motion. Chalcraft trembled and nearly required support. Mr Mann ascended the platform and addressed on their behalf an excellent prayer, at which Chalcraft became very agitated, and his fellow*

Godalming Meadows, site of the execution of Chennell and Chalcraft. Sam Milner

prisoner somewhat moved. No appearance of a design to confess being noticed, the platform was drawn from under them, and they were both launched into eternity. They both seemed to struggle when thrown over, but the executioner soon terminated their sufferings by drawing down their heels with great force.

Their bodies were placed back in the wagon and the procession continued through the town of Godalming to the house of George Chennell senior. The corpses were then taken to the very same kitchen in which Elizabeth Wilson had been murdered, and there they were dissected by two Godalming surgeons, and left exposed to the view of the thousands who queued to view the horrific spectacle of their mutilated bodies. Justice was seen to have been done.

CHAPTER 11

All Go Together: The Deaths of Martin and Stephen Bromley
1958
... their deaths were the product of a deeply distressed and desperate mind.

Diana Marion Bromley, wife of a senior member of the Home Office and daughter to Sir John and Lady Pratt, murdered her two young sons Martin, aged thirteen, and Stephen, aged ten. The killings were carefully planned and even carried out with a strange sort of tenderness. This was not an act of spite or rage and these were not habitually abused children; rather their deaths were the product of a deeply distressed and desperate mind.

On Tuesday, 16 December 1958, Martin and Stephen Bromley came home from their boarding school in Deal to begin the Christmas holidays. The family always spent school vacations at their home in Inval, Haslemere. They occupied the east wing of The Croft House, an old building that had been divided into two separate wings some years previously

Headline from the Surrey Advertiser. Surrey Advertiser

THE SURREY ADVERTISER AND COUNTY TIMES SATURDAY FEBRUA

Prosecution case against Mrs. Bromley
ACCUSED OF MURDERING HER TWO SONS

ALLEGATIONS that Mrs. Diana Marion Bromley gave barbiturates to her two sons, carried them to the garage and attempted to kill them with carbon monoxide poison from a car exhaust were made by the prosecution at a special sitting of Godalming county magistrates at Guildford on Wednesday. When she found they were still alive, said Mr. M. J. Jardine, prosecuting for the Director of Public Prosecutions, Mrs. Bromley strangled one and drowned the other, cut the boys' throats, then cut her own throat and attempted to drown herself in the lily pond.

The countryside around Inval. Sam Milner

and which stood in its own grounds. It was the ideal place for a thirteen-year-old and a ten-year-old, and the boys must have felt the usual sense of excitement and anticipation that generally mark the start of the Christmas festivities. Just a little more than a week to go before Christmas Day.

Stephen had arrived home with quite a bad cough and his mother immediately put him to bed. She knew he would need to take some sort of medication to get well for Christmas, and perhaps it was this that gave Diana the opportunity to carry out the dreadful scheme she had formed. The boys would not know what tablets they were taking and, of course, they had total trust in their mother. It would have been easy enough to persuade Martin, the elder of the two, to take a similar dose to his brother as a preventive measure, or even to slip something into his bedtime drink. So on the evening of 17 December she gave both boys not cough medicine, but barbiturate tablets. They awoke the next morning feeling dizzy and nauseous, but she gave them a second dose later that day shortly after lunchtime. She did not want them to be awake for what was to follow.

That Diana had doubts about her plan is apparent. She and the boys were scheduled to have family friends for lunch at The Croft House on Thursday, 18 December. At eight-thirty in the morning she telephoned the friends to cancel the arrangements, using Stephen's cough as an excuse. Pamela Royds remembered taking the phone call from Diana. A few minutes later Diana called her friend again, suggesting that they should come after all. At ten o'clock she phoned yet again, on this occasion talking to George Royds, Pamela's husband. He recalled Diana cancelling the arrangements for a second time, despite his urging her not to, but all she would say to him was, 'No, I don't think you had better come.'

The west wing of The Croft House was occupied by Miss Hilda Woods. She called round to see the Bromleys on the morning of 18 December, and found that the boys were not well. Stephen was sick, and Diana explained to her neighbour that Martin too was starting to feel sickly. This, of course, had very little to do with the cough. Miss Woods suggested that they should see a doctor as soon as possible, but Diana was adamant that this was not necessary. When Miss Woods saw Diana again later that morning she asked after the boys but was told that they had the 'flu; Diana strongly advised her against trying to see them at all. Miss Woods left to go into Haslemere and that was Diana's cue to make her preparations.

The housekeeper, Mrs Bradbury, was not expected at work that day, and although the gardener, Mr Moorey, turned up for work as usual in the morning, Diana asked him if he would mind changing to the following day instead. He went home but a short time later received a telephone call from Diana asking where the key to the back door of the garage was kept. He explained that it was kept on top of the doorframe on the garden shed and Diana seemed quite satisfied.

While the boys slept upstairs Diana made up a bed at the back of the garage and reversed the car in. She then carefully carried the boys down one at a time and laid them on the bed behind the car. She turned on the engine, lay down beside them and waited for them all to die. In her words, 'I thought we would all go together with the car.'

She waited. Nothing seemed to happen. She waited some more. The garage grew darker as daylight failed and still Diana waited for death to take her and her sons. She checked the boys to see if they were dead and found that they were still breathing. If she had only known, the car fumes were beginning to take effect; a post-mortem examination revealed that Stephen's blood was saturated to twenty-five per cent with carbon monoxide, and Martin's to thirty-two per cent, but Diana was unaware of this. She thought that she would have to find another way of ending their lives before they regained consciousness. She took a cloth belt, tied it firmly round Martin's throat and strangled him. It must have required an enormous physical effort on Diana's part and rather than repeating the same procedure on Stephen, she carried him to the bathroom, filled the bath with water and held him under until he drowned. The boys looked dead but before she made any attempt to join them herself she had to be sure they were not just unconscious, so she took a razor blade and slashed their throats until there was no chance that either one of them had survived.

Now it was time to kill herself. The razor blade was still in her hand and with this she inflicted a gaping wound about three inches long in her own throat. She bled but not enough to satisfy her that she would die of the injury, so with a piece of rough string she tied a heavy brass object round her neck and went to the lily pond in the garden. Her frustration deepened as she realised that the pond was not going to be deep enough to drown in. Dripping wet, bleeding and now in deep, deep distress she walked back in the direction of the house.

At about eight o'clock that evening Mr Moorey the gardener found Diana Bromley leaning on the gate in the grounds of the house, not far from his cottage. She was shivering in the sharp December chill and he was very concerned at her state. In the cover of darkness he was unable to see the wound to her throat, but he could see that both her hair and her clothing were wet and that she was wearing no coat. The weather was cold, windy and rainy, and he urged her to go back to the house as soon as possible. She seemed unable to respond and so he urged her in again, this time accompanying her as far as the driveway to the house. He went straight home and told his wife, Doris, about Mrs Bromley's strange behaviour. Doris felt very uneasy and decided to pay a visit to Miss Woods, Diana's immediate neighbour. The two ladies discussed the situation and felt that they really should pay a visit to the east wing of the house just to make sure all was well.

They found the lights on in the Bromley's home but no one was around. The ladies called out and on receiving no reply decided to check the rooms of the house. They did not think to look in the bathroom where Stephen lay drowned, but, to their great alarm, they did see quantities of water and blood in the downstairs cloakroom. Given that Mrs Bromley had specifically asked for the key to the garage earlier in the day, they next looked there, but any attempts to see in were thwarted by the firmly locked doors. The two women returned to Mrs Moorey's cottage to consider what to do next.

There was nothing for it; they would have to return to the east wing of the house. As anxious as they were about what they had seen for themselves and what they had heard about from Mr Moorey, they had no real cause to bring in outside help at this stage. When they went back for the second time the garage doors were wide open and Diana was standing in the entrance, wet, shivering and, in their words, 'in a dreadful state'. Their first concern was for Diana herself and they strongly recommended that she should go upstairs to change into some dry clothing. At the very suggestion of going upstairs Diana's agitation increased, and she seemed determined to keep the women downstairs. 'No, no, you mustn't go up there,' was all she would say. It was then, as she moved into the light, that the two ladies saw the wound on Diana's throat and the 999 call was finally made.

When Mr Bromley arrived home from work late that evening it was to find his life in shreds. Martin lay lifeless in a carefully made bed at the back of the garage, Stephen still lay in a bath overflowing with water upstairs and his wife sat at the kitchen table, a gaping wound to her throat and in a state of deep shock. A local doctor, Dr Roland Milton, had been called to the scene and dressed Diana's injury as well as he could, after first confirming that, in his opinion, both boys had been dead for several hours. Diana was taken to Haslemere and District Hospital, where, in the words of the local newspaper, 'treatment was given throughout the night to save her life.' It was, however, blatantly a life that she did not want to be saved.

All evidence led to the unthinkable; that a loving and respectable mother had deliberately taken the lives of her own sons. When charged Diana simply stared at the police officer,

Detective Inspector Cornish. She told him she had given the boys some blue tablets, Tuinal, but when asked why she did not reply. She just sat staring at him. She answered a few more basic questions, and Detective Inspector Cornish asked her what she remembered. 'I remember cutting myself with a razor blade near the washbasin,' she said. He asked her if there was anything else. 'Stephen to the bathroom,' she said, and then fell silent. The police officer had the experience and understanding to sit quietly, and wait for her to talk in her own time. 'I remember going to the little pond to drown myself and tied a brass thing round my neck to keep me under. I got right in the pond, but it wasn't deep enough. I think the car engine must have stopped and that's why we were still alive.' She sat quietly for a moment or two but then the enormity of what she had done must have hit her with force, and she became extremely upset.

Diana was remanded in custody at Holloway Prison and made at least three appearances in court at Guildford. Possibly because there was more physical evidence linking her to the death of Martin, she was initially charged only with his murder. During the hearings she sat motionless.

She was scheduled to appear in court again in the second week of January 1959 but was unable to attend because of 'a serious illness', according to reports in the newspapers. The illness turned out to be the result of another suicide attempt made on 7 January. The senior medical officer at Holloway, Dr Mervyn Williams, advised the court that it might be three to four weeks before she would be fit to make an appearance. Her trial opened at the Surrey Assizes on Wednesday, 25 February and Dr Williams once again addressed the court. He stated that in his opinion Diana Bromley had been suffering from 'melancholia and was insane' and he revealed that on three previous occasions she had received treatment at a mental hospital. In the course of her most recent bid to kill herself, deprivation of oxygen had resulted in some degree of brain damage. She was now suffering from memory loss and was unable to understand anything other than the simplest instructions. She was found unfit to plead, and although her dreadful actions can never be justified, it must truly be hoped that her loss of memory shielded her to some extent from the horrors of that tragic day.

CHAPTER 12

The Norman Massacre: No Bloodier Deed Was Done
1036

By the first light of morning his men were led into the open countryside, their hands bound and their feet shackled in chains.

In the year 1036 a massacre took place in Guildford that was so brutal it shook even the hardened sensibilities of the Saxons. It was talked of for decades and according to the *Anglo-Saxon Chronicle,* 'nor was a more bloody deed done in this land after the Danes came'.

The political tensions that led to the massacre are complex and to understand them fully it is necessary to trace events back over the preceding years. King Cnut had held the English throne for nineteen years before his untimely death in 1035. He had established relative peace out of chaos, but his unexpected end threatened to throw the country back to the turbulence of former days. He left two principal contenders for the throne: Harthacnut, favoured by most as his legitimate and therefore rightful heir, and Harold Harefoot, an older but illegitimate son. If Harthacnut had been present in the country at the time of his father's death, then the succession would probably have passed smoothly on to him and the issue would have been instantly resolved. But he was not; instead he was busy in Denmark defending the family homeland from the aggressive attacks of King Magnus of Norway. Harold Harefoot, on the other hand, was in the right place at the right time.

It was imperative to establish some solid leadership in England as soon as possible, and so, in Harthacnut's absence, the Witan elected Harold Harefoot to hold temporary power until his half-brother could return from Denmark to take the throne for himself. Although this was probably the best solution available to them, it immediately split the country into two factions: those who wanted permanent power for Harold Harefoot, and those who wanted Harthacnut to return as soon as possible to take over from his half-brother.

Harold soon showed signs of wanting to hold onto the throne for himself, and since possession gives the immediate advantage, it was greatly feared by his opponents that he would never give up the reins of power to anyone else. But Harold did have some formidable opponents, and among them were two key players in the events that were to follow: Earl Godwine of Wessex, and Queen Emma, King Cnut's widow. Earl Godwine was one of the greatest magnates in the land, and he was an ardent supporter of the absent Harthacnut. Queen Emma, Harthacnut's mother, was obviously going to do everything in her power to protect her son's inheritance.

So the scene was set in eleventh century England for an almighty struggle, and the players worked to place themselves in the most advantageous position for the support of their favourite. Queen Emma took herself off to Winchester, the capital of Wessex, and waited impatiently for the arrival of her son from Denmark. Harold, in a display of power, sent his men to Winchester to deprive the dowager queen of any treasure she might still be holding in the name of her late husband, Cnut. It was an obvious act of aggression that made Emma feel vulnerable, despite the protection of powerful men like Godwine. And so she turned for support across the Channel, to her two sons from a previous marriage, the Athelings Edward and Alfred.

Before her marriage to Cnut, Emma had been the wife of King Ethelred, known to history as Ethelred the Unready. His title, though, is misleading. It comes from the Old English 'unraed' meaning 'no counsel' or 'poor counsel' so that in his day Ethelred was known more for being ill-advised than for being ill-prepared. Ethelred's reign was, however, spectacularly unsuccessful, and he eventually fled to Normandy leaving the country severely weakened. But he had two sons by Emma, and before he died he took them into exile with him, and in Normandy they stayed until summoned by their mother in her hour of need more than twenty years later.

Emma sent word to her young, but now grown-up sons in Normandy, explaining to them how she was being treated by Harold Harefoot, and how he was threatening to usurp the throne of their younger half-brother, Harthacnut. As loyal sons, the brothers discussed how they could best help their mother and at the same time defend their family's interests.

It was a time of anxiety and insecurity in the country. When news of the athelings' plans to visit their mother became known, some were deeply suspicious. Were they really coming merely to support their mother, or did either one of them have plans to make a bid for the English throne for himself? The young men did, after all, hold a claim. They were the sons of an erstwhile king and princes of the royal house of Wessex. Indeed their title, atheling, refers to precisely that. Derived from 'aethele' meaning 'noble', and 'ing' meaning 'belonging to', the term 'atheling' was used in early Saxon times to describe anyone of noble birth, but in later years its use was reserved for those nobles from the house of Wessex. It is difficult to reconstruct the events of so long ago with any degree of certainty, and some historians still regard the visit of the athelings as an attempted invasion, but there is no real evidence to support the idea that either of the princes was making a serious attempt to take the throne of England. By no stretch of the imagination could their meagre entourage be seen as an invasion force.

There is even divided opinion as to whether both brothers set out from Normandy or just the younger, Alfred. Some reports state that Edward came first via Southampton to see his mother a short distance away in Winchester but that his arrival was opposed by local forces and he immediately withdrew. Other sources suggest that he successfully met with Emma but left when events started to turn sour. A contemporary history written specifically for Queen Emma, the *Encomium Emmae Reginae*, says that only Alfred came. He crossed the Channel from Boulogne after visiting his brother-in-law in Flanders, and marched with his armed escort travelling west from the coast along the Ridge Way towards Winchester.

The Encomium Emmae Reginae. By permission of the British Library

Alfred and his men were intercepted by Earl Godwine and under the ostensible protection of the earl and his army, they marched together towards the town of Guildford. What were Godwine's true motives here? Was he advising the atheling to hold open negotiations with Harold Harefoot, who, even as acting king, held enormous power? Was he being careful to protect Harthacnut's right to the throne, even from his half-brother, Alfred? Or did he intend all along to lead the atheling into a trap?

The party arrived at Guildford, an important centre of commerce and communication even back in the eleventh century. The town marked the intersection of the Ridge Way, a long established

Queen Emma and her sons. From the Encomium Emmae Reginae. By permission of the British Library

thoroughfare for travellers, and the more recently constructed route leading south from London. It even had a mint where silver coins bearing the head of King Ethelred and Edward the Martyr were struck. The town's status was reinforced by the presence of a castle, a timber structure on a raised mound protected by a wooden stockade. Within the perimeter of the castle lay an assortment of outbuildings and on the outside the tradespeople of the town had built their own more modest dwellings.

The fyrd, or local militia, was summoned to welcome the Norman party and on the night of their arrival in Guildford Alfred the Atheling and his men enjoyed the finest traditional Saxon hospitality. Mead and ale flowed freely, the food was plentiful and the Saxons and Normans enjoyed open camaraderie. At the end of the evening the visiting Normans were split into small groups of tens and twenties and billeted in the outbuildings within the stockade. Earl Godwine himself withdrew to his own lodgings and distanced himself from the unseemly events that followed.

In the early hours of the morning the unsuspecting Normans were woken in their billets to find blades held to their throats. Their weapons were confiscated and they were bound in chains. From this moment Alfred the Atheling was left completely unprotected. By the first light of morning his men were led into the open countryside, their hands bound and their feet shackled in chains. Here, with no regard for either judicial process or military custom, they were mutilated, tortured and most of them ultimately killed. But it was the manner in which these men died that shocked contemporaries so deeply. The Normans had shown no signs of any aggressive intentions and up to that moment had been treated as honoured guests; but even if they had suddenly been cast in the role of enemy, as soldiers they deserved at least a clean and honourable death. But here they were, bound and defenceless in the face of their captors, trapped by means of subterfuge and forced to endure not only the fear and pain of their present fate, but worse than that, the disgrace and humiliation of a dishonourable end. Still in their chains they were made to sit in rows, then some were blinded, others scalped, some

Guildford showing the Mount. Surrey History Centre

attacked with spears and others beheaded. Only one man in ten was spared, and it is likely that even these survivors were subsequently sold into slavery.

The site of this massacre may well have been the hill now known as The Mount overlooking Guildford. In 1929 archaeologists discovered there the remains of some 200 bodies, the hands still tied and many of them horribly mutilated. But whether or not these were the skeletons of the murdered Normans, written records leave us in no doubt of the outcry caused by this atrocity. The *Encomium Emmae Reginae* is, of course, bitterly critical of these events, and leaves its judgement to history in this way:

> *hence all ages will justly call such torturers worse than dogs, since they brought to condemnation the worthy persons of so many soldiers not by soldierly force but by their treacherous snares.*

Alfred himself was not harmed during the massacre at Guildford. However, he was taken prisoner and removed to the monastery at Ely, and on the journey his captors plucked out his eyes. He later died of his wounds. The *Encomium* avoids giving any details of his ill-treatment to spare the feelings of his mother, Queen Emma, but cannot resist implying that the young man's sufferings were very great. 'As I write my pen trembles,' the manuscript reads, 'and I am horror-stricken at what the most blessed youth suffered.' It is entirely possible that there never was any clearly defined intention to kill Alfred, but merely to render him powerless.

But who was actually responsible for this massacre? Once more opinion is sharply divided. The *Anglo-Saxon Chronicle* clearly accuses Earl Godwine. When describing Alfred's journey to Winchester it states that, 'Godwine hindered him, set him in captivity, and drove away his friends, and killed some of them in different ways.' Indeed Godwine was later forced to stand trial for the offence during Harthacnut's reign, and his defence was that by taking Alfred to Guildford he was offering his protection, but that other troops had taken the men captive without his knowledge. The implication was, of course, that these other troops belonged to Harold Harefoot. So at the very least, then, Godwine had turned a blind eye to the massacre, if indeed he did not actually deliver the men directly to their executioners. But why should such a powerful man risk being even remotely involved in this bloody deed? The answer may go back as far as King Ethelred, the father of the athelings. Under the rule of Ethelred, Godwine's family had lost most of its lands, and since that time the earl had worked tirelessly to rebuild the family fortunes. He would have felt very reluctant to risk his estate in the event of either of Ethelred's sons taking the throne. Harthacnut, son of Cnut, he supported: the athelings, sons of Ethelred, he most certainly did not.

The *Encomium* is careful not to blame Earl Godwine, but points the finger directly at Harold Harefoot. It describes the massacre in this way:

> But after they had eaten and drunk, and being weary, had gladly ascended their couches, behold, men leagued with the most abominable tyrant Haraldr appeared, entered the various billets, secretly removed the arms of the innocent men, confined them with manacles and fetters, and kept them till the morrow to be tortured.

At one point even Queen Emma was accused of being complicit in the murder of her own son, an accusation she vigorously denied. One tale has her undergoing the ordeal of walking across red-hot plough shears in the courtyard of Winchester cathedral in order to prove her innocence. It seems highly unlikely that she would have played any part in plotting the death of Alfred, but she may have felt a certain amount of guilt in calling him to her assistance in the first place.

Harold Harefoot did indeed take the throne of England for himself in the year following the Guildford massacre. His five-year reign was judged as disastrous and ended when Harthacnut eventually came to claim his birthright. On Harthacnut's death Edward the Atheling, elder brother to the late Alfred, having bided his time in Normandy, came to claim the throne for himself. He became known as Edward the Confessor, and it was as a result of his close ties with Normandy that William the Conqueror later laid claim to England in 1066.

The Saxon tower of St Mary's, Guildford. Sam Milner

CHAPTER 13

The Wigwam Girl: The Brutal Death of Joan Pearl Wolfe
1942

The body, in advanced stages of decomposition, belonged to a young female ...

With the Second World War in the full throes of activity in 1942, army training was crucial, and this alone excuses the military authorities for turning the outstanding natural beauty of Hankley Common into the rutted wasteland of a mock battlefield. Mounds of churned-up earth lay in the wake of the many tanks that rumbled mindlessly across the beauty of the wilderness, the remains of camps built for overnight shelter disturbed the peace of the woods, and tyre tracks crushed the heather in dark, wavy lines.

In addition to accommodating the established British camps, Hankley Common was the temporary home to a large number of American and Canadian soldiers who were receiving their military training in preparation for action. On Wednesday, 7 October 1942 two Royal Marines, William Moore and Jack Withington, were on a routine foot patrol across the common. It was Moore who noticed, protruding from a mound of earth that had been disturbed by the tracks of earlier vehicles, what appeared to be an arm. Closer inspection revealed the existence of a foot some feet away,

The mound where Joan Pearl Wolfe's body was discovered. Surrey Police Archives, Mount Browne

Close-up view of the mound showing the arm and foot protruding from the earth.
Surrey Police Archives

suggesting that a body lay buried in a shallow grave linking the two grisly finds. They disturbed nothing but immediately reported the discovery to their NCO back at camp. The police were informed and within twenty-four hours they had brought in forensic experts, Dr Eric Gardner from Weybridge and Dr Keith Simpson of Guy's Hospital, to take charge of the scene.

The body, in the advanced stages of decomposition, belonged to a young female and the stench was overpowering. Maggots and flies crawled over the rotting remains. The doctors and officers on the scene needed a strong stomach to complete their assignments and it was a day few of them would ever forget. It looked very much as though the young girl had lain dead in the woods for between four to six weeks. She was still fully clothed, lying face down in the mud, and her right arm was outstretched as though she had been dragged some distance by this arm and just dropped where she was found. Her green summer dress, tied about the waist with a rough piece of string, covered shabby underwear. Her headscarf had fallen to her neck, on her feet were colourful ankle-socks but her shoes were only discovered later some yards away.

The decomposing body of Joan Pearl Wolfe. Surrey Police Archives, Mount Browne

Her injuries were appalling. Firstly, she had received a heavy blow to the face, fracturing her cheekbone and knocking out a tooth. It is conceivable that this injury was the result of a heavy fall, perhaps caused by one of the many trip wires concealed throughout the area. There were stab wounds to her skull and to her right arm and hand, indicating that she had been attempting to defend herself. The wounds must have been caused by a very particular type of implement; muscle and tendon protruded from the gashes as though pulled out by a hook-shaped knife and it looked as though it had been difficult to withdraw the weapon from the flesh. Her right foot displayed more jagged cuts, possibly caused while the body was being dragged across the heath land. And lastly the damage to the back of her skull was extensive. The fractures spread right across the cranium and a section of bone at the back was entirely missing. In Dr Simpson's opinion these cranial injuries had been caused by a heavy, blunt weapon, such as an iron bar or pole and were the most probable cause of death. It was his later view, when he was able to carry out a post-mortem, that the blow to the back of the head could also have crushed the cheek into the ground, explaining the facial fracture. As a final indignity, small woodland animals had eaten away at the parts of her body that had been left exposed.

Although the girl's face was damaged beyond any possibility of recognition, pathologists were able to give a basic description of the victim to enable the police to trace her identity. Examination of the bones placed her age at between eighteen and twenty; although at least one tooth was missing, it was possible to see from the angle of her jaw structure that her teeth must have protruded slightly; she was approximately five feet four inches tall, had fine, mousy, chin-length hair and was petite. There was not enough of her uterus remaining to enable the pathologist to say whether or not she was pregnant at the time of her death.

In the days following the discovery, Hankley Common was searched for evidence, a difficult task given the extent and nature of the terrain. Apart from her shoes, several other articles were found, some of which gave the police the lead they were looking for. There was no sign of the hooked knife, but a birch pole was discovered several hundred yards from the body. It was more than three feet long, and, weighing more than two and a half pounds, it was considered a likely candidate to be the murder weapon. Her missing tooth was found just beneath the surface of the soil, along with the missing section of bone from her skull and a handful of hair. Then various small articles that must have belonged to the dead girl were found; a rosary, a crucifix, a bible, soap, a white elephant mascot and a green purse. More revealing than anything, though, was a letter, apparently written by the girl to her Canadian boyfriend, and signed 'Joan'. In the letter Joan explains that she is once again in hospital, more because she is pregnant and has nowhere else to stay than because of an actual illness. She writes with eagerness about their forthcoming marriage, and begs the unnamed boyfriend to tell her as soon as he has permission for the ceremony to take place. She ends the letter:

Write soon, Darling, and keep smiling for soon we will be together for always, and if you cannot get permission to marry me now I will wait for you until after the war, and then we will be. But I hope we will be married very soon because of the baby, and because I love you more than anything else in the world.

It was all the police needed. The girl was identified as Joan Pearl Wolfe, a nineteen-year-old who had gained a reputation as something of an eccentric in the area. She originally came from Tunbridge Wells but had left home in 1939 or 1940 to find work in factories; she ended up in the Guildford area, choosing to spend most of her time around the army camps. She was known locally as 'the wigwam girl' because, being too poor to get accommodation, she lived in a tent-like structure built for her on the common by her boyfriend. The next task for the police was to track down this boyfriend, and it did not prove to be too difficult.

Various people remembered seeing the strange young girl in the company of a Canadian soldier from the Jasper Camp at Witley. Three detectives paid a visit to the camp on 12 October and interviewed twenty-nine-year-old Private August Sangret of the Regina Rifles. After showing him various articles of clothing belonging to Joan Wolfe, police reported that, far from making any anxious enquiries about his girlfriend's whereabouts, Sangret instead replied, 'I guess you have found her. Everything points to me. I guess I shall get the blame.' A damning response if ever there was one.

August Sangret was a Métis, a half-breed French/Cree Indian, from Battleford, Saskatchewan. His education was

Woods around Whitley. Sam Milner

rudimentary, at best, and his home was likely to have been marked by signs of deprivation. His signature on formal documents is shaky and ill-formed, as though he were incapable of writing. He spent his early working life as a farm labourer, and for four years was a member of the local militia, the Battleford Light Infantry, the obligations of which were to undergo two weeks' military training each year. He had enlisted with the Regina Rifles in 1940.

Sangret was interviewed extensively by the police. It took more than three days to take down his statement and in the course of this, the nature of his relationship with Joan was revealed. The two had met on 17 July 1942 in a pub in Godalming. By the end of that same month Joan was admitted to hospital after fainting in the street, and in a letter written from her hospital bed she told Sangret that she was pregnant. He promised to marry her. On her discharge from hospital she had nowhere to stay, and it was at this point that August Sangret built Joan her little 'wigwam' in the woods, a simple wooden structure made of branches and furnished with little more than Sangret's army issue cape and several army blankets. By the end of the month of August, Joan had lost her job and the authorities insisted that she move from her hut near the camp. Sangret built her another shelter, this time slightly further away, and the couple enjoyed a brief period of romance in the woods, at least according to Joan. She wrote of their time in the woods in a letter from the hospital, reminding Sangret of the good times they had shared:

> *Gosh, I was never ill when you looked after me, and I was happy anyway. I will never regret what we have done, and we have had some good laughs, and tears too. (Oh! burning wood, the loveliest smell in the world.) I will never forget that, will you?*

But the path of their affair was certainly not a smooth one. It was not acceptable to the army authorities to 'keep' a woman near the camp and at one point Joan was moved on by the military police and Sangret himself placed under arrest. Joan wrote to him, mortified that he was being punished on her account and saying that the blame should all be hers. She writes:

I did not sleep much, thinking about you being shut up in the Guard House, and if you missed me too, and hoping and praying that you will not get into too much trouble, because if it had not been for me you would never have slept out or taken any military property. I should be the one to get into trouble, not you, and they did not say anything to me.

Whether or not Sangret was actually able to read these letters from Joan is in doubt, but presumably he would have been able to find someone to read them to him. Joan was once again admitted to the Warren Road Hospital in Guildford, but she appeared at his camp again at the beginning of September. She moved into an old burnt-out cricket pavilion owned by the Thursley cricket club, and Sangret slipped out of the army camp at night to join her there, returning in the early hours of the morning. They were regularly meeting there at the time of Joan's death.

In her letters Joan sounds passionate and deeply in love, but it seems that she was not the only woman in Sangret's life and he was not the only man in hers. She swore to him that she was faithful, and that may have been true in the strictest sense, but she certainly spent time with other soldiers. She had become a 'camp follower' at the age of sixteen, running away from home to go to Aldershot before moving on to Guildford. Her mother wrote to her repeatedly, begging her to mend her ways, to return home and to get herself cured (from VD it later emerged). While living in her hut on Hankley Common she certainly saw other men, among them a Czech soldier from the Sudetenland, an American soldier and at least one other Canadian. When they had first met she told Sangret that she was engaged to be married to a Canadian soldier named Francis, and there is a distinct possibility that the baby carried by Joan, if indeed there was a baby, was his and not Sangret's. And she does, in fact, mention Sangret's jealousy in her letter; was this a possible motive for murder?

Sangret claims that one day Joan simply did not turn up at their makeshift home in the cricket pavilion. Given that on several other occasions she had been taken into hospital, it is possible he assumed the same thing had happened again. He mentioned her disappearance to two of his comrades. He also told these same friends that he and Joan had quarrelled about a woman who sent him parcels from Canada. Did he believe that she had perhaps run off with another soldier of her acquaintance as a result of their quarrel, or did he know that she was already dead?

It seems that Sangret did attempt to track down Joan. On the night of 14 September, the day of her disappearance, he left his friend, Joseph Wells, in the course of an evening's drinking in public houses in Thursley, to go to the pavilion to look for her. She was not there. He left again a while later, searching for over half an hour. When he left a third time, now in the dark, Wells went with him and the two spent some time calling out her name, but to no avail. He told another friend, Patrick Anderson, that he thought Joan must have gone home to Tunbridge Wells. But still he tried to find her. The following day, Tuesday, 15 September, he went to see a Miss Hayter, a lady with whom Joan had lodged for a brief period. Miss Hayter's evidence at Sangret's trial was somewhat confused, but she said that Sangret had come to see her in search of Joan, and all she was able to tell him was that she thought she was married to a Canadian called Francis; Sangret knew this not to be true. He told Miss Hayter that he was going to marry Joan and that he was very fond of her. He then went looking for her in Godalming and Guildford.

The next person Sangret turned to was the sergeant in charge of the Regimental Police at Jasper Camp. Sergeant Harold Redvers Wade had shown some sympathy for the couple's situation, even though it had been his job to discipline Sangret for having kept a woman on army land. Sangret explained that Joan had disappeared and asked for the sergeant's advice. Wade probed a little further into the circumstances of Joan's disappearance, asking the private about their quarrel. Sangret admitted that during the course of the argument Joan had accused him of not really wanting to marry her, to which he had replied, 'No, I don't.' To the sergeant the situation seemed straightforward; Sangret did not want to marry the girl and she was no longer around to trouble him. Where was the difficulty in that? Sangret then confessed that that was not the reason he had sought the sergeant's help. In Wade's words, 'Upon that I asked him why he had reported it, and he said that if she was found, and anything had happened to her, he did not want to be mixed up in it.' Sangret was, it seems, the master of the unfortunate response.

After his initial interrogation by the police, Sangret was returned to the army camp. At about the same time one of the drains in the guardhouse, the one leading from the washrooms, became blocked, and after a few weeks of unsuccessful attempts to clear it, the drains were given a thorough inspection. The cause of the blockage was then discovered; it was a clasp knife that had been pushed into the U-bend, and more significantly, it was a clasp knife with a hooked blade. The history of the knife was quickly established. A fellow soldier, Private Samuel Crowle, had found it in the trunk of a tree near to Joan's shack. The army police in their turn gave it back to Sangret and it now looked very much as though he had tried to dispose of it in the drains. When questioned by the civilian police about the knife, Sangret denied any knowledge of what had become of it.

With the discovery of the knife, coupled with the possibility of traces of blood on Sangret's battledress and blankets, the police felt they had enough evidence to make an arrest. The uniform and blankets had been washed and this made it difficult to state categorically that the stains on them were of human blood but it was enough to turn suspicion in the direction of the Canadian private. When charged Sangret denied the murder, even suggesting that Joan might have committed suicide, but ended by saying, 'Someone did it and I will have to take the rap.'

August Sangret was tried at the Surrey Winter Assizes on Wednesday, 24 February 1943. Evidence was placed before the jury, and exhibits such as the knife, clothing, the letters, the birch pole thought to have crushed her skull, and, quite shockingly, the victim's skull itself were all brought into the court. Witness after witness told of the strange love affair between the couple in the woods, and the story of their brief time together was reconstructed. Also reconstructed, in theory at least, was the manner of Joan's death. First came the stab wounds, they surmised, repeated thrusts to the head that were terrifying in their intensity. Her arms were raised defensively and took more thrusts from the hooked knife. She tried to run away, bleeding and most likely screaming too, down the hillside over the rough terrain of the heath land. As she fled she dropped her handbag, the contents scattering as it fell. When she reached the bottom of the hill she either tripped over one of the many trip wires laid by the army, or was knocked to the ground, and there she was struck with the birch pole. She stood no chance whatsoever against the crushing weight of the makeshift club, and her skull was pounded into the ground until she was dead.

It was evident from the infestation of maggots that she must then have been crudely covered, possibly by no more than a blanket, and left for several days. Her assailant, or at least someone, then found her body, dragged it by the arm to the mound where she was discovered, and buried her under a shallow covering of earth.

One of the last to take the stand was August Sangret himself. He refuted some of the minor points on which certain witness statements conflicted with his own. The evidence against him was circumstantial, and this fact was reflected in the judge's summing up. He instructed the jury that the verdict of manslaughter was not open to them, as the girl had quite obviously been murdered. 'The only question you have to determine,' he continued, 'is: Have the Crown satisfied you beyond all real doubt that the prisoner, August Sangret, is the man who murdered her?'

The jury was satisfied in this respect. Two hours after retiring to consider their verdict, the jury returned to declare the prisoner guilty, but put forward a strong recommendation for mercy.

Although the trial of a half-breed French Canadian raised little interest at a time when the events of the Second World War dominated the news, subsequent reflection on the trial of August Sangret has raised some debate. Macdonald Critchley in his book *The Trial of August Sangret* feels that the case is a landmark for forensic science, but does not seem to doubt the validity of the verdict. M J Trow in *The Wigwam Murder* takes a more questioning approach. Does Sangret's suggestion that Joan may have killed herself demonstrate his stupidity, or does it hint at his innocence? Only someone who was unaware of the nature of the appalling injuries to the back of Joan's skull could even imagine they were self-inflicted. And, he argues, there were other men in Joan's life and no one seems to have considered them as possible killers. While it could obviously have been a pretence, Sangret did try to find Joan after her disappearance, and Trow suspects that he did find her, or at least her body. This does not mean that he must have been the killer, but that he found her and gave her a hasty burial on the mound of earth. It would explain his enigmatic response on first being questioned; 'I guess you have found her. Everything points to me. I guess I shall get the blame.' There were thousands of potential suspects on Hankley Common at the time of Joan's murder, and Trow is not convinced that the right man was convicted.

On 29 April 1943 August Sangret was hanged at Wandsworth Prison, his hands tied behind his back, his ankles fastened together, and a white bag placed over his head. It was during the term of office of Albert Pierrepoint, and although Sangret was not mentioned in Pierrepoint's autobiography, it is more than likely that the famous executioner carried out the hanging with his usual efficiency. All that remained of the love affair between the 'wigwam girl' and her Canadian soldier was the graffiti Joan had scratched into the walls of the Thursley cricket pavilion just before her death. Among other doodles and scribbles she wrote, 'A. Sangret – Canada – J. Wolfe now Mrs Sangret – England – September 9th 1942.' And beneath it was a child-like drawing of an idyllic house, entitled 'Our Little Grey Home in the West.'

CHAPTER 14

Milford Poisoning: The Slow Death of Marjorie Radford
1949

... *she complained of feeling very ill after eating the food*

The realisation that Frederick Radford was slowly poisoning his wife, Marjorie, came just too late to save her life in April 1949. The true cause of her suffering was masked by the fact that she was already dying of pulmonary tuberculosis, so that the staff of the Surrey County Sanatorium in Milford, where she died, cannot be judged harshly for not recognising the symptoms of arsenic poisoning. At the time of her death Marjorie weighed less than five stone, and in her system was a total of six and a half grains of arsenic. The average fatal dose is just two grains, but examination showed that the poison had been administered over the course of the previous fourteen to seventeen weeks.

Marjorie was admitted to the hospital in May 1948 after having been taken ill the previous Christmas. In 1949 Radford began sending his wife special treats like pies, jellies, custards and fruit, and at a time when food rationing was still strictly enforced, this was indeed a generous gesture. However, in most instances he would not take the food in himself, but

Headline from the Surrey Advertiser. Surrey Advertiser

Doctor ate arsenic pie sent to kill woman in hospital
MURDER PLOT IN LABORATORY

A DOCTOR in charge of a hospital, finding a parcel containing fruit pies on his desk, "somewhat unwisely" ate a small piece before he read the letter sent with them. In a few minutes he was ill. The pies contained arsenic. Similar poisoned pies had been given to a woman patient in the hospital by her bigamous husband. She died, and the husband committed suicide when the police began to inquire into her death.

instead sent it to her via her father, James Kite. James, who had lived with his daughter and Radford in their home in Sanderstead, visited her often. On one occasion he took some jelly and custard prepared by Radford, and she complained of feeling very ill after eating the food. The following week she refused a similar offering, so James took it home again. This time Marjorie's eldest son ate the jelly and was so ill he had to stay in bed for two or three days.

Frederick Radford. Surrey Advertiser

The food continued to arrive. It was natural to assume that anyone suffering from tuberculosis might feel unwell, but Marjorie became very suspicious of the food sent to her by her husband, as she was ill with such regularity after eating it. Eventually, in April 1949, she confided in a friend, Lilian Formby. She showed her some fruit pies and some plums and said, 'I think Fred has done something to my food.' She had eaten just one quarter of one of the tarts and been violently ill.

Lilian took the remains of the food with her and sent them in a parcel to Dr Reginald Allison, medical superintendent at the hospital. She sent a covering letter with the tarts, but because the matter was so sensitive she had marked the envelope 'private and confidential'. Dr Allinson happened to be away for three days, and so the food was left in his office. But the covering letter, because it was marked as confidential, was kept safe so that it could be handed to him personally when he returned. This was how Dr Allinson came back from his long weekend away to find the tarts in his office with no immediate explanation of what they were or who they were from. He assumed they were a gift for him and ate some of the pastry. Fortunately for him, he only ate a little. Within two hours he was violently sick, and continued to feel unwell until the following day when he received the letter and understood what had happened. He immediately informed the police.

The suspect food was sent for testing at the Metropolitan Police Laboratories where it was examined by Dr George Turfitt. He found a total of four grains of arsenic in the pies and one and three quarters in the plums. The results came back on 12 April, but sadly just too late for Marjorie; she had died that very afternoon.

This case is complex and full of enigmas. Why exactly did Frederick Radford feel the need to murder a woman who was already dying? There is no evidence to show that this crime can be viewed in the light of a mercy killing; Frederick was not known for his kindness to his wife. In fact Radford himself put the very same question of the police. 'Why should I kill my wife when I knew she was going to die anyway?' he asked Inspector Crowhurst. 'With my experience I would not have been such a fool as to give her the arsenic; the police would always find it.' Radford gained his 'experience' as a laboratory assistant at St Thomas's Hospital, Godalming. He had worked in chemical laboratories since training in the Royal Army Medical Corps, and now, at the age of forty-six, was in charge of ordering chemicals, including poisons, for the hospital laboratories. So was his question a double bluff?

MRS. LILIAN FORMBY
'*I took one and three-quarters o* *t* *e pies home . . .*"

Lilian Formby. Surrey Advertiser

On a more personal level, Radford's life was something of a mess. He had married Marjorie in 1935 after having met her when they both worked for a firm of manufacturing chemists. They moved together to work at another laboratory in Runcorn, Cheshire, and had what was described by Radford's father as 'a seemingly happy marriage', both being committed to raising their two sons. But during his interview with Inspector Crowhurst, Radford admitted to having had more than one affair. The first was with a woman in Chatham in 1940 who threatened to expose certain details of Radford's past. These threats pushed Radford to attempt to take his own life with an overdose of pheno-barbitone tablets. He began another affair in October 1947 with a woman named Ena Evans and this continued off and on up to the time of the investigation into Marjorie's death. The relationship appears to have been quite serious and marriage was discussed. So was Radford trying to hasten Marjorie's end so that he could marry his mistress? A letter written in January 1948 and given to the police by the lady in question might support this theory. In it Radford writes of his desire to make Ena happy, presumably he means by marrying her:

> *You have asked me to do something that I would give my life to do and that is to make you happy. And by what I have been told by Dr Campbell and the medical officer at Milford Sanatorium, it will be possible in a very short time.*

The police did investigate the possibility that Radford's mistress had played a part in Marjorie's death, but found nothing to implicate her. The Coroner, at the inquest, stated:

> *She has been very much interviewed by police, but I have not brought her before this court – and she may consider herself fortunate in that – because I am quite satisfied she had no knowledge of anything leading to Mrs Radford's death.*

Was impatience to remarry Radford's motive then? It would seem more than likely, but there was another secret in Radford's past that complicated matters even further. It was possibly this secret that Radford's first mistress had threatened to expose in 1940.

The marriage between Frederick and Marjorie Radford in 1935 was bigamous. A previous wife, Evelyn, whom Radford had married in 1926, was still alive. The couple had one daughter, born three years later, but Radford had walked out on the marriage in 1929, shortly after the birth of the baby. The police were satisfied that Marjorie herself had had no knowledge of this, even at the end of her life. The burden lay squarely on Frederick Radford's shoulders.

This burden clearly proved too heavy for Radford to bear. He was called for interview by the police on Friday, 15 April. At first he tried to lie his way out of the situation, but the police already had enough information to catch him out. He finally admitted to having bought the poisoned pies, but refused to admit to having tainted them with arsenic. But he was very distressed and began to realise that the evidence was against him. However without a confession, the evidence gathered so far was considered insufficient to make a formal charge. Reluctantly the police drove Radford home to his rooms at St Thomas's Hospital, Godalming. On the morning following this interview with the police, Frederick Radford was found dead in his bed. He had poisoned himself with a dose of prussic acid, in the words of the Coroner, Dr J Murray-Robertson, 'a more merciful death than arsenic'. He left a letter, rather sadly addressed to no one in particular, which read:

I am just tired of being badgered about for something I know nothing about. The stuff that has been found in my wife's body is as much a mystery to me as to anyone else. It has nothing to do with me, I don't know anything about it. I also know that things look black against me, but there you are, I have tried to do my duty, but apparently have failed. All the best – F. G. Radford

On 19 May 1949 the inquest jury returned the verdict that Frederick Gordon Radford had murdered Marjorie Kite, also known as Radford, by arsenic poisoning, and had then killed himself with a dose of prussic acid.

CHAPTER 15

Baby Killing: The Newborns
1901, 1919 & 1931

Infants were simply abandoned in woods, in fields, in any quiet corner, and these unfortunates were referred to as 'dropped babies.'

Today we take it for granted that both babies and mothers normally survive the ordeals of childbirth, and that children will be loved and cherished in all but the most extraordinary of cases. Reports of child abuse and infant death are nowadays met with genuine horror. But such expectations were not always met in the past. The death of a child in the first ten years of its life was a more than common occurrence. In the second half of the nineteenth century the deaths of children up to the age of five accounted for more than forty per cent of all deaths in some heavily populated urban areas. It would be foolish to assume, though, that because it happened more frequently it was a less painful experience. The grief of parents has always been, and always will be, of the deepest kind.

The babies at greatest risk were those born out of wedlock. It was estimated that in Victorian manufacturing towns up to thirty-five per cent of illegitimate children died before the age of one year, and that figure jumped to a shocking seventy five per cent in London. Not all those deaths were natural.

The killing of babies, especially illegitimate babies, was a frequent crime, even in the early twentieth century, and newspaper reports regularly gave only a brief account of such a common phenomenon. But before we are tempted to look back in judgement, we need to understand the social pressures that many of the unfortunate young mothers had to face.

The options for girls, often in domestic service, who found themselves both pregnant and abandoned by the baby's father, were very limited indeed. Those lucky enough to have supportive families might return home to have their baby and then resume work leaving the child with its grandparents. Very few indeed would have found sympathy from their employers. They would be turned away from their work, usually with little or no money of their own. Then the options were to live on the streets, to earn a living as a prostitute or go to the workhouse. Dickens gives us an idea of the appalling conditions of the workhouse in his journalistic writing. Unmarried mothers would share squalid conditions with the old, infirm, sick and insane. He concludes that:

> *We have come to this absurd, this dangerous, this monstrous pass, that the dishonest felon is, in respect of cleanliness, order, diet, and accommodation, better provided for, and taken care of, than the honest pauper.*

Many young girls went to desperate lengths to conceal their pregnancies and dispose of their babies. Infants were simply abandoned in woods, in fields, in any quiet corner, and these unfortunates were referred to as 'dropped babies'. The newspapers are flooded with examples of such cases, in most instances not warranting more than a line or two of comment.

In April 1919 the naked and decomposing body of a newly born girl was discovered on a dust heap in Haslemere. The mother, Harriett Roe, an unmarried domestic servant, was traced and charged, not with murder, but with concealment of birth. She admitted that she had told no one of her pregnancy, and the typical style of dress for servants made concealment easier than one might imagine. She gave birth to the baby girl in the lavatory of the house in which she worked, and since the child had made no sound, had hidden the body in a bucket until she was able to dispose of it on the rubbish heap. Because of the advanced state of decomposition of the body, the court was unable to prove that the child had had a separate existence, and the judge decided that Harriett should be bound over on her own recognisance, 'to give her an opportunity of redeeming her past'.

More sinister were the baby farms run by unscrupulous women who charged a fee to desperate young mothers for 'taking care of' their babies. It was tacitly understood that the babies would, more often than not, simply die of neglect and starvation. The exposure of one Surrey baby farm hit the headlines in 1919. Mrs Flitter, aged sixty, and Mrs Bell, aged forty-one, appeared at the Surrey Assizes charged with the deaths of two babies, and with the wilful neglect of seven others. The first of these babies to die was Allen MacDougall at just fifty-five days old. The doctor who examined his body described him as 'pinched and emaciated' with 'the face of an old man'. Following the post-mortem it was reported in the *Surrey Advertiser* that:

> *He* [the doctor] *found it mere skin and bone, and its legs were drumsticks. There was no disease, but a complete absence of fat.*

All the children under the supervision of Mrs Flitter and Mrs Bell were of unmarried mothers, their so-called care having been paid for in a lump sum or in weekly payments ranging from 8s 6d to 10s. Both women were sentenced to eighteen months imprisonment without hard labour, and the children were taken to the workhouse infirmary, where it is uncertain that they would have fared a great deal better.

In other instances there was little doubt that the infants were murdered at birth, or shortly after, by their own mothers. Perhaps the panic-stricken young girls persuaded themselves that it was a kindness compared to the hostility and deprivation the children would face if they lived. Perhaps they were simply afraid for their own fate. The newspapers then were littered with reports of dead infants, and the authorities in many cases were remarkably lenient.

The crime of infanticide was punishable by death until 1938 but such a sentence was rarely given. It was generally accepted that women suffered from extreme mental instability following the birth of a child and that they were not responsible for their actions. More often than not the charge was reduced from murder or infanticide to the lesser charge of concealment of birth, even in the face of overwhelming evidence that the babies had been deliberately killed. And the punishment, too, was surprisingly light.

In January 1901 twenty-three-year-old Edith Raggett was arrested on a coroner's warrant at the Guildford Union Infirmary for the wilful murder of her male child. She made no reply to the accusation. She had taken up employment as a domestic servant only days earlier at Elm Dene, Croft Terrace, Godalming, the home of Mr Henry Bunning. But the deed might well have remained undiscovered had she not been accused of theft, from her new employer. Because of the alleged theft police made a thorough search of her room and found a bag of bloodstained linen tucked away between the bed and the mattress. Their suspicions now aroused, they extended their search to the adjoining lumber room where Edith had been heard walking about in the middle of the night of 7 January. There PC Galloway found a paper parcel rather poignantly hidden beneath a child's cot. Inside, very carefully wrapped in a woman's apron, was the body of a newly born male, a piece of lace knotted tightly about its neck.

The post-mortem revealed that the baby was both fully and well formed, and that the cause of death was strangulation. The swelling around the neck indicated to the two doctors conducting the examination, Dr Huie and Dr Bond, that the ligature had been tied about the neck before the baby's death. They admitted the possibility that the lace might have been knotted around the baby's neck before it was fully born, but they felt this was unlikely. All indications were that the baby had breathed before it died, but Edith denied the charge of murder.

Despite the evidence, at her trial early in March that same year, the charge of murder was reduced to that of concealment of birth. And even of this the jury found her not guilty since she had been open and cooperative with the police investigation. The *Surrey Advertiser* reported that, 'the verdict was received with applause which was instantly suppressed.'

Thirty years later, well into the twentieth century, Mrs Winifred Waddell, of Brookdell, Onslow Village noticed that her servant Emily Broom, also twenty-three years old, appeared to be gaining weight. She questioned the young girl, known to her mistress simply as Broom, but Emily denied that anything was amiss. She had been working for Mrs Waddell for just thirteen months, and in that time had shown herself to be a hard and conscientious worker. Emily was an orphan, her mother having died two years previously, and her father two years before that.

During the early hours of 18 April 1931 Emily gave birth to a 7lb 10oz baby boy. The first that Mrs Waddell knew of this was at seven thirty in the morning when she heard a loud bang followed by Emily calling to her through her bedroom door, saying that she had had a baby during the night and that she was going to die. The young servant then collapsed on the floor. Mrs Waddell at once sent for both a doctor and a nurse, and, as soon as she could, asked Emily to explain what she had done with the baby. Emily swore that the baby had been dead at birth, that she had tied a piece of string around its neck and placed it in a suitcase beneath her bed. Mrs Waddell found the baby boy in the suitcase, a piece of ribbon concealing the string. Emily, under the care of a nurse now, begged to be allowed to die.

At the inquest, held at the Guildhall in Guildford on Monday, 21 April 1931, Dr J K Milligan, a police surgeon, gave evidence relating to the post-mortem examination of the baby. He stated that in his opinion the baby had died of asphyxia caused by the ligatures on the neck, the ligatures consisting of a double length of string wound and knotted round the baby's neck. On the likelihood of the baby's having had a separate existence before death, Dr Milligan gave his opinion that since the baby's lungs were expanded and contained air, it was likely that he had lived for some minutes at least, although he felt this could not be proved. On 22 April a further post-mortem was carried out at the Royal Surrey County Hospital, Guildford, by Dr R C Matson. Based on the expansion and condition of the baby's lungs, he too felt it likely that the child had had a separate existence.

Emily Broom was charged with infanticide at Warren Road Hospital, Guildford, on the day of the birth, and when cautioned said nothing but, 'yes'.

She was brought before the Guildford Borough Police Court on Wednesday, 11 May, where she sat in the dock, neatly dressed with her head bowed, and in the words of one reporter, 'appeared to take little interest in the proceedings'. Based on the evidence, Emily was committed for trial at the Surrey Assizes. As an employer Mrs Waddell appears to have been more caring than most, as she offered to stand surety and to take Emily back into her home. All that was to no avail though, as Emily was denied bail and was remanded in custody in Holloway Prison. In the magistrates' opinion it was in her own best interests not to be allowed back to the home of Mrs Waddell, and they expressed their belief that she would be well looked after in Holloway.

By the time Emily appeared before the assize court judge in July she had decided to plead guilty to having caused the death of her baby son. Her defending counsel placed her sad circumstances before the court. As an orphan she not only had no one to support her, but since her mother's death she had worked to support her two brothers and three younger sisters. Her record up to that point had been blemish free, and Mrs Waddell gave evidence as to her good character. Even the judge acknowledged that the situation must have been 'a horrible nightmare for the girl'. However, in spite of the fact that Mrs Waddell was keen to take Emily back into her service, the judge decided that a custodial sentence was required. The magistrates may have been mistaken in their estimation of how well she would be cared for in Holloway Prison, because as the two-month gaol sentence was passed on her, Emily Broom was taken from the dock screaming.

CHAPTER 16

A Father's Shame:
The Death of Frederick Martin
1919

*From the kitchen she heard a strange noise,
like a muffled scream ...*

By the summer of 1919 the Martin family had been living in Midleton Villas, Midleton Road, Guildford for eight years. Caroline and Frederick Martin had just one child, a boy named Freddy after his father, and although Frederick senior had recently been unwell, their lives carried on in a generally steady and contented fashion. By most normal standards of the day they would have been seen by friends and neighbours as a happy family.

Freddy, who would be thirteen in a month's time, was a bright, young boy. He attended Sandfield Boys' School where he was due to be transferred to the seventh standard after the summer holidays; he had played the piano since he was seven years old and he also sang in the Stoughton Church Choir. His favourite pastime at home was making wooden models of boats.

Frederick Martin senior was thirty-seven years of age and Caroline a few years younger. Frederick worked as a motor fitter, and was a quiet, well-read man, private but by no means reclusive. The family had not been away for a holiday that summer, and Frederick tried to make up for this by taking them all to a performance at the Paddocks Pavilion, a local theatre, and by promising Freddy that he would buy him a bicycle.

On the afternoon of 12 August 1919 the family of three sat down after lunch feeling replete and restful. Father and son had spent a companionable morning together at an auction in the Cattle Market, hoping to find a reasonably priced bicycle.

Now the sun was pouring through into the front room, and Caroline noticed that her husband seemed brighter than usual. He had been dealing with some health issues, but said that he was feeling much better that day. She suggested that they had a short rest, and since the front room was so bright with the summer sun, all three took books and magazines upstairs to lie down in one of the back bedrooms. At the last minute Caroline thought it would be a nice touch to round off lunch with a cup of tea, so she left her husband and son reading on the bed while she went downstairs to put the kettle on.

From the kitchen she heard a strange noise, like a muffled scream, the sound of movement and then nothing. In alarm she rushed upstairs to find her husband standing in the bedroom and Freddy trying with difficulty to get off the bed and head towards the stairs. She was unable to make proper sense of what she saw. There was blood everywhere and she moved to help Freddy, taking hold of him and supporting his weight since he appeared to be unable to do so for himself. She half carried him towards the stairs; he seemed determined above all things to reach the stairs. He collapsed, and unable to bear his weight by herself, she had no choice but to let him fall to the floor of the little landing on the bend of the stairs. In her words, 'There seemed a mist over his face.' It was then that fear caught up with her and she cried for help, jumping down the remaining steps and running out of the house, terrified and bewildered in equal measure. In her panic, what she had not fully taken in was that Freddy's throat had been slit.

Mrs Greenway was the first neighbour to respond to Caroline's cries for help. She guided the hysterical mother to the green opposite the cottages, where Alfred Cook, another neighbour, was enjoying the sunshine. At the same time Charles Kenyon, the next-door neighbour, also arrived at the scene. 'See what's the matter with him. See what he has done with him,' cried Caroline, unable to explain what had happened. 'I tried to bring him with me, but he would not come. Do you think he will die?' Unsure of what to expect, the two men went into the house and found Freddy lying in the crook of the stairway, face down with his head resting on his left arm. He was dead. As the men carried the young boy down the stairs they saw that his throat had been cut. The question now uppermost in everyone's mind was the whereabouts of Frederick Martin senior. The men searched all the rooms in the house for him but he was nowhere to be seen. They did, however, see a trail of blood that led from the bedroom to the kitchen, and then on to the downstairs lavatory. The door was locked and so Mr Kenyon stayed to keep watch while Mr Cook ran to telephone for both a doctor and the police.

Detective Constable Manfield arrived at Midleton Villas by five to four that afternoon. He saw the body of the young boy lying on the mat by the front door, and as he moved through to the back of the house noticed a great deal of blood on the floor of the scullery. Lying in the blood was a carving knife. The police managed to open the lavatory door, and inside they found Frederick Martin senior, alive but unconscious and bleeding profusely from a cut to the throat. They pulled him out at once, bound the wound with a clean towel and arranged for him to be taken with all possible speed to the County Hospital in Guildford.

The police officers then searched the rest of the house. Understandably they found a lot of blood on the bend of the stairs and on the bedcovers, but the bedroom bore no signs of having been the site of a struggle. If the father had indeed cut his own son's throat before slashing his own, and there seemed no other possible explanation for what had happened, then he must have taken Freddy utterly by surprise. The act had to have been premeditated though; one does not have a carving knife fortuitously to hand in the

Headline from the Surrey Advertiser. Surrey Advertiser

DISTRESSING TRAGEDY AT GUILDFORD.

FATHER MURDERS SON AND ATTEMPTS SUICIDE.

MOTHER'S TERRIBLE ORDEAL.

OPENING OF THE INQUEST.

Woodbridge, Hill, one of the newly developed outlying districts of the town, was the scene of a terrible tragedy on Tuesday afternoon, when a man named Frederick William Martin, living at No. 3, Midleton-villas, Midleton-road, attacked and murdered his 12-year old son with a carving knife, almost severing the head from the body, and afterwards turned the weapon upon himself and attempted to commit suicide by cutting his own throat.

bedroom, and, as confirmation of this, the police found a cut-throat razor, opened at an angle of forty-five degrees, hidden beneath the bed. No suicide note was found.

Dr Hilda Adams, house surgeon at the Guildford County Hospital, assessed the extent of the wounds to Frederick Martin's throat. The injury was indeed severe, the cut severing virtually everything in front of the larynx and incorporating damage to the external jugular vein. The lacerations would have to be sewn up as quickly as possible, but she had every reason to hope that his life could be saved. However, as the anaesthetic was about to be administered, Frederick Martin said just three words: 'Let me die.'

Caroline was understandably distraught and the women of the neighbourhood rallied round her. She could not return to her own home, so vivid was the memory of the horrifying scene, but she went to stay with her sister, who lived in the same road. After conducting a painstaking search of the premises, the police locked up the Martin's house, leaving it bloodstained and empty. It was, of course, left to Caroline to arrange the funeral of her son. It took place the following week at the Emmanuel Church, and after the service the party of mourners went to Stoughton Cemetery, where the choir sang 'On The Resurrection Morning' as the coffin was lowered into the grave. The moment must have been achingly poignant for Caroline, as the one face missing from the choir was Freddy's.

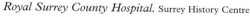

Royal Surrey County Hospital. Surrey History Centre

But the question still remained: why had Frederick Martin killed his only son? From the investigation that followed two possibilities emerged: an overwhelming sense of shame, or madness. Frederick Martin had been suffering from syphilis, and his GP, Dr Arthur Brodribb, gave his evidence in court. The doctor had treated Frederick Martin for syphilis in the third stage in 1910, but in the doctor's opinion he had been cured. Nonetheless, despite the passage of almost a decade, the shame of having contracted the disease was still with Frederick Martin in 1919.

He was due to undergo an operation for haemorrhoids, and he was very distressed at the thought that his previous illness might be discovered in the course of this operation. He questioned Dr Brodribb about this on more than one occasion, and the dread of discovery played heavily on his mind. It is important to understand the social stigma attached to this illness at the turn of the twentieth century. It was only after the publication of the Royal Commission Report in 1916 that special clinics were established to offer both free treatment and confidentiality for patients. The treatment, too, had progressed. Previously, mercury had been the only treatment available, but since the identification of the micro-organism responsible for the illness in 1905, new methods of dealing with it were being researched. In 1909 a new treatment became available, Salvarsan, a compound of arsenic, administered through intramuscular injections. But the illness remained shrouded in misinformation and disapproval.

It is possible that Caroline may have been unaware that Frederick ever had syphilis and, as strange as that may seem in the twenty-first century, it is entirely in keeping with attitudes of the period. The medical profession considered it advisable to keep wives in the dark about such delicate matters, leaving it to the consciences of men not to infect their wives. There was also some element of confusion about the method of transmission of the illness. It was understood that it was transmitted via intercourse, but many people thought it could also be transmitted by normal daily contact. Perhaps this was why Frederick Martin took Freddy to see the doctor earlier that year to see if any traces of the illness could be found in him. Although the doctor reassured the father that there was nothing to indicate that Freddy was infected with the illness, Frederick remained concerned. It is true that the illness can be passed to an unborn infant by an infected mother, but in those cases the symptoms become apparent early in the baby's life. Was Frederick Martin aware of this? Or did he believe that by killing both himself and his son he would be eradicating any evidence of his guilty secret?

The other possibility is that the illness itself may have induced dementia. At the trial, the medical officer from Brixton Prison, Dr G Griffiths, described Frederick Martin's general medical condition. The injury to his throat had impaired both his ability to raise his head and to speak; the knife wound had damaged the tongue muscle making words slurred and difficult to understand. Martin was in a generally depressed state, which might have been expected, but his mental functions also appear to have been affected. He found it difficult to follow conversations, and he had a dull, vacant look in his eye. It was the doctor's conclusion that, '[Frederick Martin] had syphilis of the brain, and was in a fairly early stage of general paralysis of the insane,' and that, 'the alleged act was committed whilst he was in the maniacal state.' Fortunately Frederick Martin retained only a hazy recollection of what he had done to his son. In the doctor's opinion he was unfit to plead and there was no real option but for the jury to find him insane, given the medical evidence. Therefore the judgement was that he was to be detained at His Majesty's pleasure. The judge gave permission for his wife and brother to visit him before he was taken away, but whether Caroline chose to take advantage of this offer is unrecorded.

CHAPTER 17

Popular Justice: The Hanging of Christopher Slaughterford 1709

... he hurled himself into oblivion, refusing to wait a second longer for that fatal push

Born in Westbury, Surrey, in the last quarter of the seventeenth century to an honest farming family, Christopher Slaughterford's early life was exemplary. He served his formal apprenticeship on a farm in Godalming after which, according to the Newgate Calendar, 'he served some other farmers in that neighbourhood with great fidelity and always bore the character of an inoffensive young man, neither keeping bad company, nor being addicted to any sort of extravagance'. He worked hard and saved enough money to settle himself in a malt-house in Shalford, where he made a good business for himself. His aunt kept house for him and his prospects for the future looked good; he would have made an excellent catch for any of the young working girls in the neighbourhood.

But Christopher Slaughterford's eye turned in one direction only; towards an attractive young servant girl by the name of Jane Young. Although Jane's family was poor, she had raised her own prospects by obtaining a position as domestic servant to a gentlewoman, Elizabeth Chapman. She seems to have been happy in her position, but like all young women at that time looked forward to the day when she had a home and family of her own. And so she was more than content to receive the attentions of a young man in Christopher's position. Neighbours often saw the two of them together in the homes of mutual friends or walking side by side in the surrounding countryside. All seemed proper, and the courtship was apparently progressing so well that in October 1708 Jane Young informed Mrs Chapman that she would be leaving her post in order to get married. Her mistress wished Jane well and spent some time admiring the new clothes that Jane had saved up for in readiness for married life. The future must have seemed rosy indeed for the young servant girl.

But it was not wedded bliss that fate held in store for Jane; instead, her life came to an abrupt and mysterious end. Her lifeless body was found floating in a pond not far from Slaughterford's house in Shalford. A surgeon carried out an examination and discovered several wounds to Jane's head; this, apparently, was no unfortunate accident, but was starting to look distinctly like a murder.

The local farming community was outraged at the death of one of their own, especially when it was the death of a girl who had so much to live for. Christopher's reaction to the death of his fiancée has never been recorded. If, as we might imagine, he was grief-stricken, it would not have suited the purposes of the neighbourhood to acknowledge it, for they were determined to blame him for her death. Again in the words of the Newgate Calendar, 'a clamour was raised against him, and every person believed that he had murdered her.'

There was no real physical evidence to indicate who had killed Jane Young, but the local community began to construct their own theories, theories that frighteningly quickly became accepted as fact. He must have seduced her, they surmised, and then wishing to discard her after ill-using her, had disposed of her in the most brutal fashion. We do know, however, that Slaughterford was vehement in his denials of any involvement with or knowledge of Jane's death. But the accusations built up to near hysteria, and no one seems to have even considered the possibility that Jane's murderer might have been a stranger passing through the district.

In an attempt to establish his innocence Christopher Slaughterford voluntarily surrendered himself to the authorities. A local justice of the peace listened to all the evidence against him, but had no hesitation in dismissing the case and ordering Slaughterford to be discharged.

If he had hoped that this would end the matter, then Slaughterford had misjudged the depth of his neighbours' fury. People now began to repeat damning statements said to have been made by Slaughterford himself, statements that implicated him in Jane's death.

One woman claimed that she had asked Slaughterford what had become of his whore, to which he was supposed to have replied, 'I have put her off; do you know of any girl that has money your way? I have got the way of putting them off now.' Another said that before the murder was even discovered she had asked Slaughterford what he would do 'if Jane Young should lay such a child to you as mine here'. She claimed that he sighed deeply, declaring that that was now impossible, before breaking down in tears. These two accounts seem contradictory in that the first portrays Slaughterford as callous and mercenary, the other as deeply regretful. Then a male neighbour claimed to have seen a man and a woman walking together on the common at three o'clock on the night of the murder, and that the man was dressed in light coloured clothing similar to those owned by Christopher Slaughterford. He did not say that these people were definitely Christopher and Jane, he merely implied it, but it was enough to add fuel to the growing speculation. After he had passed the couple, he said, he heard a scream. If this were true it is interesting that he apparently did nothing about it. Even the surgeon decided that the injuries to Jane's head were of the right size to match a stick owned by Slaughterford.

Slaughterford's aunt and the young apprentice who lived in the malt-house with them, both swore under oath that he had remained in the house the whole of the night of the murder. Slaughterford presented himself to the authorities once again, this time to a bench of magistrates. In the face of such a public outcry it was decided that the case should be heard at the next assizes, and until that time Slaughterford should be held in custody at Marshalsea prison.

At his trial witnesses were heard, and the case presented before judge and jury. Christopher Slaughterford was found not guilty of the crime of murdering his fiancée, Jane Young. At last he could return home to rebuild his life, or so he thought. As much as one might suppose that the question of his innocence had been resolved, the matter did not end there.

The Newgate Calendar takes up the story:

Such was the malice of the people, or such was the notion they had of his guilt, that they advised the father of the young woman, rather than suffer him to escape, to lodge an appeal at the Queen's Bench Bar, in hopes of being able to convict him.

The law made provision for the heir of the deceased to bring a private prosecution. However, if such a prosecution proved successful the prisoner was unable to appeal to the Crown for mercy, since the case had not been brought by the Crown but by a private individual. So if Slaughterford lost in the private prosecution he could not escape the gallows, even though under normal circumstances, such a dubious case would have warranted an application for mercy. The case had already been dismissed by one magistrate and Slaughterford had been found not guilty by a jury of his peers, but yet again he was forced to endure the ordeal of a trial with his life hanging in the balance.

The appeal was put forward in the name of Jane's brother Henry Young, and the case was heard by Lord Chief Justice Holt, among others, at Westminster. The Young family was far too poor to bear the cost of bringing the lawsuit but the neighbours made a collection in order to help them. This time the jury, comprised of Surrey men, found Christopher Slaughterford guilty of the murder of Jane Young, and he was sentenced to die on 9 July 1709 in Guildford High Street.

The truth of this story has been lost with the death of its protagonists. Perhaps the neighbours knew more than has been recorded, or perhaps in their grief they turned their anger in the most obvious direction and

GUILDFORD JACK-DAW.   5

1at it had been the means of ftop-
ing that cruel fport of bird's-
efting. If it had been dark, I
n fure it would have checked
1em, and they would have flunk
ong like fo many thieves: for is it
3t amazing, that though a murder
1d been committed in this place fo
any years fince, and the man was
1nged at the market-houfe in the
wn of Guildford (as you may fee
the picture)

Page from the Guildford Jackdaw. Surrey History Centre

Close-up from the Guildford Jackdaw *showing the hanging of Christopher Slaughterford.* Surrey History Centre

refused to look any further. It is by no means uncommon for accused men to deny their guilt and for relatives to provide alibis for them, but this tale holds more than a passing similarity to a witch-hunt in its crescendo of accusation and hysteria. Christopher Slaughterford did indeed lose his life as a result of the private prosecution. He was the last man to be hanged in Guildford High Street, more precisely at the Market House; later executions took place on The Mount overlooking the town. He continued to proclaim his innocence to the very last moment and the strain of living under both constant accusation and the shadow of execution revealed itself in the manner of his death. As soon as the executioner had fastened the noose about his neck he hurled himself into oblivion, refusing to wait a second longer for that fatal push.

The only record of Slaughterford's own words on the subject remain in a letter he sent to the Sheriff of Guildford on the very morning of his death. It reads as follows:

Guildford July 9, 1709

Being brought here to die, according to the sentence passed upon me at the Queen's Bench Bar, for a crime of which I am

wholly innocent, I thought myself obliged to let the world know, that they may not reflect on my friends and relations, whom I have left behind me much troubled for my fatal end, that I know nothing of the death of Mistress Jane Young, nor how she came by her death, directly or indirectly, though some have pleased to cast reflections to my aunt. However, I freely forgive all my enemies, and pray to God to give them a due sense of their errors, and in his time to bring the truth to light. In the meantime I beg everyone to forbear reflecting on my dear mother, or any of my relations, for my unjust and unhappy fall, since what I have here set down is truth, and nothing but the truth, as I expect salvation at the hands of Almighty God: but I am heartily sorry that I should be the cause of persuading her to leave her dame, which is all that troubles me. As witness my hand, this ninth day of July.
Christopher Slaughterford

Tunsgate. The site of Slaughterford's execution as it looks today. Sam Milner

Chapter 18

Babes in the Wood: Leslie and Eileen Gaff
1947

It was very difficult for anyone involved with the case to control feelings of outrage and anger at the senseless deaths of two such very young children.

The two police officers who stood either side of the prisoner at the Guildford Borough Magistrates Court on 28 July 1947 watched their charge closely. The tall, fair-haired and even good-looking young man was about to come under a lot of scrutiny, considering the despicable crime for which he stood charged. Dressed in a crumpled blue suit, the twenty-one-year-old watched the brief court proceedings that day, answering simply, 'Yes, Sir,' or 'No, Sir,' when asked a direct question by the magistrate. He must have been thankful that news of his arrest had only just spread through Guildford, giving very few people time to take their place in the courtroom. Hundreds, however, were beginning to gather outside Guildford Police Station in North Street, hoping for an opportunity to express their loathing for the man being held inside. The waiting crowd was to be disappointed; Frederick Alfred Smith was ushered out of the High Street entrance of the court, his hand cuffed firmly to the escorting police officer.

The scene was rather different when the case was resumed on the following Friday. By this time the newspapers had had time to cover the story, and the headlines referred to the 'Babes in the Wood'. The courtroom was packed with spectators, and many more gathered outside the entrance. Among those sitting in the court waiting for the magistrates

Boy Found Dead in Wood: Sister Dies in Hospital

WINDOW CLEANER IN COURT

"AN ACCIDENT": ALLEGED STATEMENT

FREDERICK ALFRED SMITH, aged 21, described as a window cleaner, of 2, Bushnell Cottages, Pitch Place, Worplesdon, was charged at Guildford Borough Magistrates' Court in the Guildhall on Monday with the murder of two Guildford children, brother and sister.

They were **LESLIE JOHN GAFF**, aged nine years, and **EILEEN GAFF**, aged seven, of 196, Southway, Westborough. When they were found in woods near Manor Farm on Saturday afternoon the boy was dead; the girl died on Sunday night in the Royal Surrey County Hospital.

The two separate charges against Smith alleged that he murdered the children some time between 1 p.m. on Friday, July 25th, and 3.30 p.m. on Saturday, July 26th. He was remanded in custody, and yesterday was further remanded until next Friday.

SMITH IN COURT

"AN ACCIDENT": ALLEGED STATEMENT

Smith, who was dressed in a blue, chalk-striped, single-breasted suit which was badly crumpled, was closely guarded by two police officers during his appearance in court, which lasted only a few minutes. He is a tall, powerfully-built man, fair-hai...

who said he last saw the two children on Tuesday of the previous week in the garden of their home, whether anything was then said with regard to their meeting any particular person later that week. The answer was, "No, sir."

"Behind me sits a man charged with the murder of these two children," went on Mr. Methold. "Have you ever seen him in the company of the ...

Headline from the Surrey Advertiser. Surrey Advertiser

were two men who had a keen interest in what was about to take place; one was Frederick Smith's father, and he sat in grim silence waiting for the evidence that could lead his son to the gallows. The other was Frederick Gaff, father to nine-year-old Leslie and seven-year-old Eileen, the brother and sister allegedly murdered by Smith.

Both men had been present at the inquest held at the Guildhall in Guildford the previous Tuesday. When Frederick Gaff walked across the courtroom floor to take the stand, he shielded his eyes with his hands as he passed the accused, Frederick Smith, so repugnant was the very sight of him to the bereaved father. Mr Gaff was clearly in a very distressed state

The Guildhall, Guildford. Sam Milner

and gave his evidence before the Coroner only with great difficulty; he needed some little time to compose himself. No one who saw his anguish could have remained unmoved and indeed the inquest jury waived their fees and asked that the money should be paid instead to Frederick Gaff. Even in the midst of such overwhelming grief, a touch of kindness means a great deal.

The full hearing was postponed three times, and at the third magistrates' hearing when police asked for Smith to be held in remand yet again, the two fathers, Mr Smith and Mr Gaff, silently acknowledged the fact that each, in his own different way, was undergoing an ordeal. Mr Smith approached the father of the murdered children first, and shook him by the hand. The men then sat quietly side by side for the duration of the short hearing.

When the case was finally heard before the magistrates and Smith was

Stairs to the witness box at Guildford Court. Surrey History Centre

committed for trial at the Surrey Assizes in December, the full story of the children's deaths unfolded. They had lived in Southway, Westborough, Guildford, with their parents and twenty-year-old sister. At one o'clock in the afternoon of Friday, 25 July they left home to go out to play and took with them their father's white whippet, Snowy. They did not return home. By the evening the family was extremely worried for their safety; the children were used to playing on the local common land but had never before stayed out so late. At ten thirty-five that evening Leslie and Eileen's disappearance was reported to the police in a telephone call made by their elder sister. The police responded immediately by organising a search, but by the failing light there was little hope of finding them that night. By the first light of morning many more volunteers had joined in; the operation by this time was so extensive that police borrowed a hymn board from a local church so that they could mark out the different areas being searched using the hymn numbers, which they attached to sticks in the ground. Even a group of Girl Rangers on a camping expedition joined in the painstaking search for the missing children.

They were found on the Saturday afternoon in Dene Copse, a wooded section of Manor Farm. Leslie was dead, a bullet from a .303 service rifle having passed cleanly through his body. Just a few feet away lay Eileen with severe injuries to her head, but alive and calling out in her weakened and frightened state for 'Mummy'. Standing guard over both the children was their dog, Snowy. Someone had attempted to scratch out the name and address from the identification tag on his collar. Whoever had done it did not want the children to be instantly identified.

In his memoirs, *Friends and Villains,* the officer in charge of the investigation, Superintendent Tom Roberts, recalls how the children were finally found. It was an interesting example of acute observation. One officer involved in the search on the common, Inspector Lock, noticed that a particular hazel bush appeared to be wilting when all the greenery around it thrived; a closer look revealed that the stem had been badly damaged, as if by a bullet. And sure enough, nearby lay the body of

Leslie Gaff; the bullet, then, had not only passed through him but through the bush too.

Eileen Gaff was taken straight to the Royal Surrey County Hospital, and was operated on that night for the severe injuries to her head. Despite the best efforts of the medical staff to save her life, she died late on the Sunday night. Police were now investigating a double murder. It was very difficult for anyone involved with the case to control feelings of outrage and anger at the senseless deaths of two such very young children.

An examination of Eileen's injuries provided an important piece of evidence. Although the official post-mortem showed that she had died from shock and a fractured skull, there were some other minor wounds on her arm, and one of these showed the imprint of the rear sight of a .303 rifle stamped into the flesh. The wounds to her head must have come from a heavy, blunt instrument, and were perfectly consistent with having been inflicted by a rifle butt. At least the police now knew what they were looking for.

According to locals who knew the two Gaff children, they had been seen that day with a man known to them as 'Uncle Tom'. From this the police were able to formulate a description, and very late on Sunday night, shortly after Eileen's death, someone telephoned in the belief that he had seen a man who matched this description. The lead was followed up. The suspect was Frederick Alfred Smith, a window cleaner who was staying at that time with his brother, William, at 3, Bushnell Cottages, Pitch Place, Worplesdon. The informant, Stanley Jones, had read the description of the suspect in the *News of the World* that day, and made the connection with Smith. The police waited outside Smith's home until he returned at twenty to three in the morning, and questioned him about his activities on Friday 25 July. He claimed he had gone to 'the pictures'. The police searched his bedroom and found boots and trousers that matched the description of the man witnessed with the children, and, more significantly, rounds of .303 ammunition. Smith declined to account for these items. The rifle itself was later found in bushes on Manor Copse, after Smith had given them instructions on how to find it.

In his statement to the police Smith explained what had happened from his perspective. He had promised to take the children out shooting with a service rifle he had bought; Leslie was running ahead with Snowy, the whippet, when Smith tripped over a tree root or uneven patch of ground, and the rifle had accidentally gone off. Leslie fell to the ground; he was killed instantly. With the shock of seeing her brother lying utterly lifeless, little Eileen started screaming, and this sent Smith into a state of panic. He claims not to recall what happened next. In his words, 'I don't remember what happened after that, I must have had a blackout or something... I was worried by what had happened and that's why I went to clean windows – to take my mind off it.' The stark truth is that he must have clubbed seven-year-old Eileen about the head with the butt of his rifle, leaving her for dead. That she had at least one wound on her arm indicates that she was trying to defend herself from the man who towered over her and despite his claims of a 'blackout', Smith was sufficiently aware to think to scratch out the dog's name and address from its collar, before leaving the two children in the copse.

There is some plausibility in Smith's assertion that Leslie's death was an accident, or at least the result of carelessness, but Eileen's death was both brutal and needless. There was no other apparent motive for the crime; no evidence of any kind of sexual assault, for example, was found. But Smith did have a background of mental instability. He had spent some time in Banstead Mental Hospital after his discharge from the army.

At Smith's trial at the Surrey Assizes on 2 December 1947, he was charged with the murder of both Leslie and Eileen Gaff, but given the likely nature of Leslie's death, the judge felt that his case should remain on file. Smith pleaded guilty to the murder of Eileen. When this was announced to the court, the judge asked Smith's counsel to confirm that he understood the full implications of this. If he did, indeed, plead guilty then the judge would have no alternative but to pass the sentence required by the law; death. Smith's counsel, Mr Neve, assured the judge that the situation had been fully explained to his client. Given the gravity of the consequences, the judge once again enquired, 'He understands the position thoroughly?' Mr Neve, who, of course, had the advantage of having read Smith's psychiatric report, reassured the judge that this was the most advisable course for Smith to take. They intended to put the full history of his mental instability before the Home Secretary in the hope that the sentence would be commuted to life imprisonment. This was a gamble, albeit a well-calculated one, and the anxiety felt not only by the prisoner but also by his father sitting in court, can well be imagined. In the words of the *Surrey Advertiser*:

> *The black cap was then placed on the judge's head by his clerk, and the solemn words of the death sentence broke the hush which fell upon the crowded court. 'Amen,' said the High Sheriff's Chaplain, and Smith went from public view.*

Inspector Roberts, in *Friends and Villains*, provides us with the outline of what happened next. As confidently predicted by Smith's counsel, his sentence was commuted to life imprisonment, and he was released from prison in December 1971. He died three years later in a motorcycle accident, on the very same day that he appeared in court once again, this time on a charge of theft.

CHAPTER 19

The Deed: The Mystery of the Unknown Sailor
1786

... they attacked him, first knocking him to the ground and then bringing out their knives.

L ife at sea at the end of the eighteenth century was hard and dangerous, even by the standards of the age. Cut off from the pleasures of the land for unpredictable and often long periods, sailors lived a cramped, wet and hungry existence, at risk not just from the king's enemies but also from the elements, which wrecked or overwhelmed hundreds of ships each year. Coming ashore was a temporary release from deprivation and danger, and it was a fact of life that sailors on land were often drunk and sometimes dangerous.

It was no surprise then, in September 1786, to find Michael Casey, James Marshall and Edward Lanigon (sometimes spelt Lonigon or Lonegan), all Irish sailors on leave, enjoying some refreshment before resuming their long walk back to ship. They were travelling on the London to Portsmouth road, a notoriously dangerous route through barren, desolate countryside, and they stopped at Moushill near Godalming to spend the little that remained of their pay. There they met a fellow sailor, known to one of them from a previous voyage but whose name has been lost to history. He has become known to locals of Hindhead simply as 'The Unknown Sailor'. Whoever he was, he showed great generosity to the three villains of this story, buying them drinks at Moushill, and offering to continue his hospitality on the shared journey back to Portsmouth, or at least for as long as his money lasted. He offered up a guinea to settle the bill, no mean sum of money in those times, and this may have given the impression to his fellow travellers that he was a man of means. The party set off together. Their next stop came two miles later at the *Red Lion Inn*, Road Lane, Thursley, possibly known as *The Little Lion* at the time of these events. The next stage of the journey would be arduous, the road passing as it did over the steep incline of the Devil's Punch Bowl to reach Hindhead. They would need to fortify themselves for the road before them, and once again the unknown mariner paid for refreshments for the whole party.

Gratitude is an unfamiliar emotion to some people, because far from feeling any sense of obligation to their generous companion, Casey, Marshall and Lanigon decided to kill him and take both his clothing and his money for themselves. The light of day was now fading and on a lonely stretch of the pathway, edged by nothing more than heather and bracken, they attacked him, first knocking him to the ground and then bringing out their knives. His pleas for mercy went unheeded as they stripped him of all his clothing and plunged their knives into his defenceless body. The murderers decided to inflict two cuts each in their victim's throat so that no one would know who had dealt the fatal wound; the blame would then be shared equally. The six deep cuts left the unknown sailor's head all but severed from his body, and these mangled remains were rolled over the lip of the pathway, down into the Devil's Punch Bowl.

Unfortunately for the three sailors they were seen disposing of the body by two local men. In the now deepening darkness

Postcard depicting scenes from the murder of the Unknown Sailor. Surrey History Centre

The "Red Lion", Thursley.

Three sailors to the "Road Lane" came.
   Lonegan, Marshall, and Casey by name;
They told a tale they were quite hard up,
'Twas long since they had bit or sup.
And they walked all night and day—
Yet Portsmouth Town was miles away.
Another Sailor came along,

From the Original picture at the "Royal Huts" Hotel, Hindhead.

A smart young tar, his name unknown,
Said, 'Cheer up mates, don't be cast down,
For I'm going home to Portsmouth Town,
As you have no cash the charge to meet
I've a shot in my locker, and I'll stand treat,"
He treated them with a right good will,
And they went together on Hindhead Hill.

the men could not quite make out what was being hurled over the side of the steep slope, and fearing for their own safety they waited until the sailors had moved on before investigating. The witnesses were horrified at what they found, and hastened to the *Red Lion* for assistance. A posse of eight or nine men gathered together and left Thursley in pursuit of the criminals. They caught up with them at Rake, where the sailors were trying to sell the dead man's possessions at the *Flying Bull* public house. The arrest was lead by a soldier called Thomas Doe and after a struggle the murderers were taken into custody. Their destination was Guildford gaol, but first the men were taken to the house where the victim lay. The *Public Advertiser* of 4 October 1786 stated that, 'on coming to the house where the mangled body lay the guard insisted on getting them out of the coach to see and touch the body'. The reason for this gruesome ritual, according to local legend, was a belief that if the murderers touched their victim's body, its wounds would bleed afresh. One of the men was overcome with emotion at this point and wept openly, whether for himself or his victim we will never know, but the other two appeared to be unmoved, even bragging that they would do it again given the chance.

Casey, Marshall and Lanigon were taken to Guildford New Gaol after being examined individually by Justice Fielding of Haslemere. They were held in captivity until the Lent assizes of the following year, where they stood indicted on two counts; the first was the theft of items belonging to an unknown man. The list of articles stolen read as follows:

Postcard depicting the murder of the Unknown Sailor. Surrey History Centre

The Deed.

From the Original picture at the "Royal Huts" Hotel, Hindhead.

They reached the Hindhead Hills at last:
Amidst the heath and purple grass
That lad's blood, more purple real,
Soon was flowing down the Hindhead Hill.
Lonegan and Casey used the knife,
Marshall begged them to spare his life,
But his prayer did not avail.—

That is as Marshall told the tale.
The deed was done! They dragged along
The body in "The Punch Bowl" flung,
The knife was cleaned, the stain wiped out,
They thought all trace removed, no doubt;
And long before the body found,
They'd be at sea, and outward bound.

A green jacket, a pair of blue trousers and check handkerchief, a hat covered with oilskin, two check shirts, a blue jacket, a pair of buckles, a black silk handkerchief, a blue shag waistcoat, blue trousers [a second pair] *and divers other things the property of a person unknown in the parish of Thursley aforesaid in the said county.*

The second charge was of wilful murder of a male person unknown. Michael Casey, aged forty-two, James Marshall, aged twenty-four, and Edward Lanigon, aged twenty-six, pleaded guilty to all the charges. Two days later, on Saturday, 7 April 1787 they suffered the punishment allotted them. They were taken to Hindhead Hill, there to be hanged and gibbeted. Their dead bodies were to serve as a warning to others, so having been cut down from the gallows, they were covered in tar and then placed within a frame of metal and chain to be hung on the gibbet. This contraption was the pride of the inhabitants of Hindhead who were able to boast that their gibbet was the only one in the county to have borne the weight of three villains. It consisted of a thirty-foot high pole which supported a metal wheel eleven feet in diameter, and it was from this that the felons were suspended. The sight of the gibbet at Hindhead with its three macabre occupants must have chilled the heart of any onlooker. Some details of a spectator's view of the execution do survive; in *Hindhead or the English Switzerland* written in 1898 by Thomas Wright, he recalls meeting with the great-grandson of a woman, Mary Tilman, who was present on the day that Casey, Marshall and

Postcard depicting the arrest of the murderers. Surrey History Centre

The Arrest

From the Original Picture at the "Royal Huts" Hotel, Hindhead.

But vengeance soon was on their track,
And quickly brought the murderers back,
A shepherd chanced that way to stray
And saw the murdered sailor lay.
He went for help and gave alarms,
When all the country people arms

And fellows in the villains' wake,
They reached "The Flying Bull," at Rake,
The law's strong guardian soon was there,
And brought them back to Hazelmere,
When justice sat and law was read—
"Condemn them to be hung till dead"

Lanigon were put to death. Wright describes the scene based on the old man's recollections of his great-grandmother's version of events:

> ... *Mary Tilman, who then lived at Squire Dawson's at Pierrepont, saw the murderers executed. It was a very windy day. They were taken to the hill-top on trolleys drawn by horses. The ropes having been adjusted, and the horses whipped away, the men dropped. When dead they were put in irons, but these not fitting, the bodies were taken the same day to the Red Lion at Thursley, where a blacksmith made the necessary alterations. Mary Tilman was amongst those who followed to the blacksmiths and the crowd was so great that she pushed against the bodies, which lay on the ground, and she trod on one of the heads.*

To feel the full impact of this type of death sentence, one must have some understanding of the attitudes to death and burial at this period. What happened to a corpse after death mattered deeply in this age; a traditional Christian burial was more than just a nicety, it was a matter of profound importance. Relatives went to great lengths to retrieve the bodies of loved ones who had been condemned to the gibbet, including climbing the pole to remove the entire cage if necessary, so that the corpse might be buried. When this practice became widespread, the authorities started tarring the pole as well as the bodies to prevent anyone from climbing up. So desperate was one mother to retrieve the body of her son that she waited beneath the metal cage to gather the bones one by one as the flesh

Postcard depicting the execution of the murderers. Surrey History Centre

Gibbet Hill.   From the Original picture at the "Royal Huts" Hotel, Hindhead.

Placed in chains, and there close by   Hanging there both night and day,
The London Road to be hung on high,   Till piece by piece they dropped away;
Where travellers by coach or van   And on the spot where the foul deed was done,
All hear the tale of the murdered man,   Can now be seen by everyone:
As they near the gibbet tree—   And on that spot the travellers know,
A sight more loathsome none could see,   No heath nor grass doth ever grow.

rotted away and the bleached bones fell through the bars of the gibbet.

In contrast to the undignified end of the murderers, the victim of this atrocity was carried to a more caring resting place. Both the nature of his untimely death and his anonymity touched the hearts of local inhabitants, and they acted towards the Unknown Sailor as they might have wished others to act towards them or their loved ones. A funeral took place for the victim on 27 September 1786, and his remains were laid to rest in Thursley churchyard. A collection was made to buy a headstone to mark his grave, and judging from the intricacy of the masonry, some of the subscriptions must have been substantial. It depicts the scene of the murder, now known to locals as 'The Deed' and the lengthy inscription reads:

In Memory of
A generous but unfortunate Sailor,
Who was barbarously murder'd on Hindhead
On Sep 24th 1786
By three Villains
After he had liberally treated them,
And promised them his father [sic] *Assistance*
On the Road to Portsmouth

When pitying Eyes to see my Grave shall come,
And with a generous Tear bedew my Tomb,
Here shall they read my melancholy Fate,
With Murder and Barbarity complete,
In perfect Health, and in the Flow'r of Age
I fell a Victim to three Ruffians Rage;
On bended Knees I mercy strove t'obtain
Their Thirst of Blood made all Entreaties vain
No dear Relation or still dearer Friend
Weeps my hard Lot, or miserable End
Yet o'er my sad Remains (my name unknown)
A generous Public have inscribed this stone

The identity of the Unknown Sailor has puzzled historians and locals alike. Only one possible lead gives us any clue at all and this was investigated by Peter Moorey in his book *Who Was The Sailor Murdered at Hindhead? 1786: A Search for his Identity.* Moorey reveals the existence of a letter written to the *Farnham Herald* in 1932 by a Mrs Anne Macmillan. In it she claims that the Unknown Sailor was her father's great-uncle and that the story of his sad fate had been told down the generations in her family. She did not know his christian name, but only that he was the brother of Samuel Hardman, a soldier in the 10th Light Dragoons, and that he died leaving an unclaimed fortune of £250,000, a fortune which remains in Chancery to this day. This is an enormous sum of money, and if the story is true may point to the Unknown Sailor not being an ordinary sailor at all.

Mrs Macmillan had details of the names of the villains, and the fact that they were gibbeted. She even told of three macabre heirlooms; the middle finger bone from one hand of each of the executed men, gathered up as they fell through the bars of the gibbet, gold tipped and turned into toothpicks for

Gibbet Hill. The monument marks the site of the gibbet. Sam Milner

The tombstone of the Unknown Sailor, erected by locals of Thursley. Sam Milner

her family to use. It was a suitably demeaning use of mortal remains.

Moorey traced the records of Lieutenant Samuel Hardman of the 10th Light Dragoons in the National Archives. This gave him the lead he needed to trace the name of the elusive brother. Samuel's service records show him to have lived in Lambeth, Surrey, and so Moorey searched the baptism records for the parish of St Mary-at-Lambeth and discovered the following entry. '1752 August ye 30th Edward son of Samuel Hardman and Mary his wife.' If this was indeed the name of the Unknown Sailor, he would have been thirty-four at the time of his murder. Moorey would like to believe that his discovery of Edward Hardman has solved the mystery of the Unknown Sailor, and maybe it has, but it will be difficult to prove. The story, meanwhile, continues to capture the imagination of all those who hear it. Even Dickens refers to The Deed in his novel Nicholas Nickelby. His characters Nicholas and Smike travel on the same path as the Unknown Sailor and find the stone which marks the spot where the murder was committed:

It was a harder day's journey than yesterday's, for there were long and weary hills to climb...They walked upon the rim of the Devil's Punch Bowl; and Smike listened with greedy interest as Nicholas read the inscription upon the stone which, reared upon that wild spot, tells of a murder committed there by night. The grass on which they stood had been dyed with gore; and the blood of the murdered man had run down, drop by drop, into the hollow which gives the place its name. 'The Devil's Punch Bowl' thought Nicholas, as he looked into the void, 'never held fitter liquor than that!'

The stone that marks the spot where the Unknown Sailor was murdered. Sam Milner

CHAPTER 20

My Mate's Wife: Mrs Agnes Muriel Ellacott
1945

First he tied a rope around her neck and tried to strangle her; then he slit her throat with a razor and before leaving the cottage he turned on the gas tap of the cooker.

The friendship between George Ellacott and Dennis Nash began in 1941 when the two were serving together in the National Fire Service. Nash, then only seventeen years old, was a dispatch rider, and Ellacott, although more than a decade older, befriended the younger man. Later Dennis Nash became a frequent and regular visitor to George Ellacott's home at Gorseland Cottages, Upper Hale. George, now working as a baker's roundsman, lived there with his second wife, Agnes, and two sons from a previous marriage. Although Dennis had his own lodgings at Castle Street, Farnham, the whole family soon accepted him as one of their number, and before long he was spending at least part of every day with the Ellacotts.

As the years went by Dennis began to visit at times when he knew George would not be at home, especially when he thought there was some chance that Agnes might be at home alone. His interest in the woman who was thirteen years his senior turned from friendship to near obsession and by 1945 it was clear that their relationship had developed into a passionate affair. But the friendship between the two men continued and they spent many evenings together drinking at local pubs. Eventually George began to feel that Nash's interest in Agnes was perhaps not entirely above suspicion. Although at this point it was nothing more than suspicion, George felt it would be safer not to let Agnes spend too much

Castle Street, Farnham. Godalming Museum, previously reproduced by R Head in 'Godalming in Old Picture Postcards'

time alone with Nash. He asked Nash not to go the cottage when Agnes was there alone and Nash's reaction to this was surprisingly emotional. He cried at one point, a more unusual response in the 1940s than it would be now, and mumbled something about them finding his body on the railway line if he could not visit the house. So family events continued to include Nash, and still the two men spent seemingly companionable evenings together.

On 26 August 1945 Nash drove George, Agnes and George's father, to Southsea for a day's outing. Whether they managed to hide the tensions that were clearly pressing on the triangular relationship will never be known, but the following morning there was clearly some sort of scene between Dennis and Agnes. He paid an early visit to Gorseland Cottages, and his presence was noted by several of the neighbours. When he arrived Agnes was doing her washing. He tried to divert her from this by kissing her, but she warned him that George had told her not to let Nash stay too long alone with her. Her behaviour was hardly warm and encouraging. She might have found some welcome diversion from the round of domestic drudgery with the younger man, but she was not foolish; George Ellacott provided

Castle Street, Farnham. Godalming Museum, previously reproduced by R Head in 'Godalming in Old Picture Postcards'

her with a stable home, whilst Dennis had nothing but his car, his motorcycle and a bank account containing just £1. When Nash vented his frustration by aiming some choice language at the absent husband, Agnes seemed distant. 'Tell him yourself tonight,' was all she replied. At this Nash left the house.

He went to a nearby café to have something to drink and consider what was going wrong with his relationship with Agnes. He felt desperate at the thought of losing her.

One of Dennis's cherished possessions was a letter, written by himself, and titled, 'My Mate's Wife'. In the letter he set out his feelings in numbered paragraphs, using the word 'darling' over twenty times, and ending the letter with more than one hundred Xs. He kept the letter for over a year without sending it.

At eleven-thirty other customers at the café saw Nash stand up abruptly and leave. He leapt onto his motorcycle and was seen riding off in the direction of the Ellacott home. A little after twelve-thirty Agnes was found dead by one of her stepsons. At twelve-forty-five Dennis Nash and George Ellacott met up at their local pub for a drink, but George, of course, had no idea of the tragic scene awaiting him at home. Chillingly, Dennis most probably did.

Nash had not meant Agnes to survive his brutal attack. First he tied a rope around her neck and tried to strangle her; then he slit her throat with a razor and before leaving the cottage he turned on the gas tap of the cooker. When police questioned him later that same day he had very little recollection of the dreadful deed. 'I was just in a blackout,' he told officers, 'I just seemed to go blank.'

He was immediately arrested. But his obsession with the Ellacotts did not stop there. He wrote to George from prison, demanding to know why his friend had not visited him, and begging for at least a photograph of Agnes's grave. He seemed unable to comprehend the impact this appalling crime had had on his friend and could not see past his own grief. He even bought the burial plot next to Agnes's grave for himself, and had the bill sent to the prison. It was clear that where Agnes was concerned, Dennis Nash had lost all ability for rational thought.

For the jury, the verdict was clear. In their opinion there was no doubt that Dennis John Nash had killed Agnes Muriel Ellacott; but equally there was no doubt that at the time of the murder, he was insane.

CHAPTER 21

The Breakfast Murder: The Battering of Joseph Hollis 1809

*But instead of finding vegetables,
Sarah discovered the scene of an
appallingly bloody murder.*

At nine o'clock on the morning of Friday, 5 May 1809 Mary Wisdom sent her daughter Sarah to collect some vegetables from the cottage of her employer, Joseph Hollis. Mary had been working for the seventy-three-year-old Hollis since the death of his wife some years earlier, and provided the only domestic help the old man needed. She had been given the previous day off since Hollis had planned to go to the Guildford Fair, held every 4 May, to buy some sheep. He had told all his neighbours he was leaving for the fair before five o'clock on the Thursday morning and intended walking the few miles from his home in Compton. So on the Friday morning Mary Wisdom planned out the day's meals as usual and sent her daughter to fetch the greens. But instead of finding vegetables, Sarah discovered the scene of an appallingly bloody murder.

On the table stood a cup half-filled with coffee, and by the fire was a piece of toast on a plate. Another partly eaten slice lay on the floor next to a broken butter dish. At first Sarah did not see Hollis, but her eyes followed the butter dish to a pool of blood and on to the body of the old man, who lay face down. She ran outside immediately, and to her immense relief met James Moore, who was both a neighbour and the Compton Constable. Together they went back into the cottage and took in the full scene.

Hollis had clearly been disturbed at breakfast; his chair was overturned, and both the table and the chimney breast seemed to have been struck by a poker-like instrument. Marks of a different shape were found on the low ceiling. The body lay on the floor, the face propped up on the left arm, and it looked as though the dead man had been dragged across the kitchen floor. Moore decided that he needed assistance and so with Thomas Whitlaw, the local publican, he went into Guildford to fetch a relative of the victim and Mr Newland, the surgeon. The men then made a closer examination of the body, and it became obvious that Hollis had put up quite a struggle for such an elderly man. He had been badly beaten, with one clear blow to the right temple and a deep cut to the back of the head; his jaw was fractured in two places, his arms were badly bruised and a finger was broken. Even the steel buttons on his jacket had been crushed beneath the weight of the blows. His throat had been cut several times with an apparently blunt implement, and so savagely that the head was almost severed from the neck. Not surprisingly, the scene was very bloody indeed.

By this time other gentlemen of the village had arrived to add their opinion to the investigation and a small crowd of on-lookers gathered by the door of the cottage. Among them was Hollis's next-door neighbour, Mary Cooper. The body was turned over and beneath it they discovered a knife, lying in a pool of thickening blood. 'That's old Master Hollis's knife,' called out Mary Cooper, even though she was standing too far away to see it clearly, and it was impossible to make out any distinguishing marks on the knife as it was so thoroughly covered in blood. The gentlemen were very struck by this. They could not see how anyone could possibly tell whose knife it was, and they questioned her accordingly. Her reply was, 'I'm sure it is Master Hollis's knife for I have seen him use it many times.' Even when another penknife was discovered in the pocket of Hollis's jacket, Mary stuck to her story. 'Oh yes, Master Hollis had several clasp knives,' she explained. If her intention had been to distract attention away from the true ownership of the knife found beneath the body, Mary Cooper failed. Her haste to identify the knife as belonging to the victim did nothing but arouse suspicion.

Joseph Hollis had spent his working life in Guildford as a maltster. He had done well in his trade, and made enough money to retire more than comfortably, with two cottages in Compton, a small flock of sheep, which he put to pasture on Compton Common, and enough money to make the contents of his wallet a favourite topic of conversation. Neighbours said he would often talk about his money and even take out his purse to display the bank notes and gold-coin he kept on him. He lived in one of the cottages, and the other, adjoining it, he rented out to James Cooper, who lived there with his mother, Mary, and his seven-year-old daughter.

The relationship between landlord and tenant had never been especially good, but a fortnight before the murder a conversation between Hollis and James Cooper was overheard by Elizabeth Freemantle, a neighbour from the Alms Houses situated to the rear of the cottages. In her words, she heard the two of them, 'rather upon a wrangle'. Hollis appeared to be very angry with Cooper, and the argument turned to the non-payment of rent. Hollis threatened to evict Cooper and his family if he did not pay the arrears and Cooper soon stormed away to the upper part of the garden where his mother was working. Elizabeth Freemantle heard James Cooper tell his mother about his dispute with Hollis; she distinctly heard him say, 'I'll be damned if I care anything for the place, but I swear I'll be upsides with him, or reward him once within a fortnight.' Mary Cooper clearly understood his intentions, as her reply was, 'God forbid'. At this he turned on her, and told her that if she did not hold her tongue he would serve her the same. 'Well it don't signify,' she replied, 'no man in Compton likes him.'

Thanks to Mary Cooper's imprudent remarks about the ownership of the knife, suspicion quickly settled on the Cooper family, even though both Mary and James provided themselves with alibis for the morning of Thursday, 4 May. Mary had left home at six-thirty in the morning to set about her usual occupation of collecting the neighbourhood post from Guildford, and James left shortly after for his job at the Guildford Fair selling

THE

TRIAL

OF

James & Mary Cooper,

(MOTHER AND SON)

FOR THE

WILFUL MURDER

OF

Joseph Hollis,

LATE OF

COMPTON in the County of Surrey;

BY

Fracturing his Skull, and afterwards Cutting his Throat,

IN A

Post barbarous and inhuman manner,

WHILE SITTING AT BREAKFAST

IN HIS OWN HOUSE,

Early on Thursday morning, May 4th 1809.

Who were Tried on Monday August the 14th,

AT

Croydon Assizes,

BEFORE

SIR A. MACDONALD,

Lord Chief Baron.

GUILDFORD:

PRINTED AND SOLD BY S. RUSSELL AND CO.

(Price 1s.)

By permission of British Library

beer. He made a point of stopping several passers-by to ask them the time, claiming to be late even though his employer later testified that he arrived for work much earlier than usual. In any case their alibis were of no help to them as Hollis had made it plain that he intended leaving for the Guildford Fair before five o'clock in the morning, and since no evidence could be found that he ever reached the fair, it was reasonable to assume that he was murdered at breakfast before five o'clock on the Thursday morning. If that was the case then the Coopers were either responsible for the crime, or they must have heard the commotion next door as someone else committed it. The partition between the cottages was thin, so thin that it was possible to hear something as slight as the ticking of a clock through the door connecting the two properties. The struggle between Hollis and his attacker was substantial and would certainly have been clearly audible to his neighbours. Yet the Coopers claimed to have heard nothing.

Mary Cooper was questioned. She had noticed nothing untoward, she claimed. She had last seen Hollis on the Wednesday evening, and when she left for Guildford to collect the post the window shutters of Hollis's cottage were not yet open, so she supposed him to be still in bed, even though he had clearly stated his intention of leaving for the fair before five o'clock. She admitted that on her return from Guildford she looked in at the window, saw the butter lying on the floor but certainly not the body. She thought it strange, but supposed that,

Plan and drawing of the cottage of George Hollis. By permission of the British Library

'the cat must have drawn the butter from the table.' Any witness to the scene of the crime would know that it was impossible to peer in at the window and to see the butter but not the body, which lay just eight inches away. Her most damning admission at this point though, was that on the Wednesday evening she had specifically asked the housekeeper whether Hollis would be alone the following morning. The housekeeper, Mary Wisdom, confirmed her statement. Why would this have been of any interest to Mary Cooper? Why was it important to confirm that Hollis would be alone? It was quite likely he would have a considerable amount of cash in the house, since the purchase of sheep at the fair would require a substantial cash payment, so does this indicate that a robbery was being planned?

Based on these suspicions, James Cooper was arrested on the evening of Friday, 5 May. He answered questions calmly, his cottage was searched but nothing was found, and without any further evidence the magistrate ordered his release.

Then several pieces of evidence came together in quick succession. A poker found at the crime scene, and which matched the marks on the table and chimney breast, was identified by Mary Wisdom as belonging to the Coopers; it was part of a set and their tong and shovel were of the same style. She was also sure that the knife found under the body did not belong to Joseph Hollis, as Mary Cooper had claimed. It was later identified by John Wigman, a fellow drinker at a public house in Merrow, as belonging to James Cooper. Elizabeth Hart, who looked after Cooper's little girl, bought two pennyworth of cabbages from the Cooper's garden and discovered splashes of blood of the leaves. She went back to the garden with a neighbour, William Tice, and they found that the ground around the well was stained dark, in their words, 'as if bloody water had been thrown thereon'. Finally James Hart swore he saw James Cooper cleaning a billhook before seven o'clock on the Friday morning. A billhook, a long-handled implement with a curved blade, was thought to have made the marks on the ceiling and could also have been the weapon used to cut Hollis's throat.

On 11 May a second search was made of the Coopers' cottage. This time a round frock, of the sort worn by labourers at this time, was found in a basket. It had been washed, in fact it was still damp, and had visible bloodstains especially around the cuffs. Mary Cooper claimed the marks were dirt not blood, but the officers conducting the search thought otherwise. Both James and Mary Cooper were arrested that day for the murder of Joseph Hollis.

At their trial both denied the charges. After all the evidence had been produced against them, they were asked for their defence. They produced no witnesses; James Cooper denied any knowledge of the incident, and Mary Cooper said, 'I had no hand in the murder. I be clear enough of it.' It took the jury only fifteen minutes to find James Cooper guilty and Mary Cooper not guilty of the murder of Joseph Hollis. After the verdict was returned James Cooper was sentenced to death by hanging. The judge said:

TRIAL, &c.

On *Monday, August* 14th, at a quarter before 12 o'clock the Prisoners JAMES COOPER and MARY COOPER were placed at the Bar, when Mr. KNAPP Clerk of the Arraigns read to the Court

The Indictment,

which contained two counts,

The 1st. *That they the said James Cooper and Mary Cooper, by the instigation of the Devil and of their own malice afore-thought, did on the Morning of Thursday the 4th of May last, at Compton in the County of Surrey, make an assault on and Murder one Joseph Hollis, of Compton aforesaid, by giving him several strokes on the Head, &c. with a Bill Hook.* —2d. *That they the said James Cooper and Mary Cooper, with a Knife did cut the Throat of the said Joseph Hollis, inflicting one mortal Wound of the length of three inches, and of the breadth and depth of two inches; thereby killing and murder-ing the said Joseph Hollis.*

To this Indictment the Prisoners pleaded—Not Guilty.

The following JURY were then sworn.

JAMES TURPIN,	JOHN BRAZIER,
WILLIAM MEAGER,	THOMAS FARLEY,
BENJAMIN POTTER,	JAMES POPE,
PETER PIGEON,	WILLIAM ROLLINSON,
RICHARD MESSENGER,	NATHANIEL CASTLEDINE
JOHN PHILPS	JOSEPH KING.

By permission of the British Library

A clearer case I have never witnessed brought into court; here is Malice, Dishonesty, Revenge and Avarice, all at the bottom. No doubt your mother was morally guilty with yourself, but as by a humane verdict of the jury she is not legally.

As the death sentence was passed on him James Cooper showed no emotion, but as he was led away called out to the judge for mercy, as he was 'as innocent of the murder as a child unborn'. Even as he faced the gallows, he refused to make a confession. Mary Cooper on the other hand was questioned again after the trial, and admitted that her son had indeed been the murderer, that she had stood at the window as he struck the old man again and again, first with the poker then finishing him off with the billhook.

CHAPTER 22

Boxgrove Mystery:
The Murder of Charles Barrett
1957

*'I kept hitting him on the head;
I lost my temper completely.'*

At six-thirty in the morning of Tuesday, 22 October 1957, Miss Alice Carr, the matron of Boxgrove School, Guildford, was woken by shouting. Her bedroom overlooked the stairs that led down to the cellar known at the school as the 'boot hole'. She went out to investigate and when she reached the landing, realised that the sounds were indeed coming from the boot hole. Cautiously she walked down the steps. The shouting continued and in the darkness of the basement all she could make out was the shape of someone crouching on the floor and another figure standing in the corridor. She called out, asked what was going on, and the man in the corridor answered her. He was William Dodds, the assistant caretaker, and he told Miss Carr in a tone of distress and urgency not to come down, but to leave as quickly as she could to get some water. She did as she was told, but as she left heard cries of 'Murder, murder'.

When she returned to the cellar some moments later carrying a bowl of water, William Dodds came out of the passage to meet her, and again told her, 'Don't come down.' He went on to explain, 'Barty has had an accident. Phone for a doctor or ambulance.' 'Barty' was Charles Barrett, the resident caretaker who had worked at the school since 1912. Now aged sixty-seven he was as strong and hard working as ever, and always prided himself on his punctuality and efficiency.

Miss Carr went to wake a teacher, Mr Alan Byrne, and the two returned to the boot hole. While Alice remained at the head of the stairs, Mr Byrne went down to the cellar to see exactly what was going on. He found Charles Barrett, the elderly caretaker, lying on the floor, and William Dodds breathless and slightly bruised. Dodds then explained what had happened. He had come down as usual to start the day's work when he saw a man run up the steps from the boot hole. The man ran off in the direction of the Boxgrove Road entrance to the school. He had only a fleeting glimpse of him; he took note of his general build and the fact that he was wearing a trench coat, but beyond that he could say very little. He heard shouts of 'Help' and 'Murder' and other noises as if 'someone was being belted,' coming from the boot hole and rushed down to see a shorter, stockier man in the room, and Barty on his hands and knees screaming. At that point he heard Alice Carr calling out from the stairs and his first instinct was to keep her out of the way. As he shouted out his instructions to Alice Carr to fetch water, he knelt down to assist Barty. It was then that the man took hold of Dodds' left arm and twisted it behind his back. Seconds later Dodds was hit from behind. Now dazed and finding it difficult to move, Dodds was aware that the stocky man had turned his attention back to Charles Barrett. There was a struggle between the stranger and the elderly caretaker and there were sounds of someone being hit. Dodds admitted to being terrified by the situation, and looked about him for some kind of weapon to use for self-defence. But at that moment the intruder ran out of the boot hole, and Dodds said he watched him turn right as he got to the top of the stairs.

By the time Mr Byrne arrived the man had fled. The ambulance and police were on the scene in a very short time, but Charles Barrett was pronounced dead on arrival at the Royal Surrey County Hospital. The police now issued a

FOUND BATTERED TO DEATH

FELLOW CARETAKER CHARGED WITH MURDER

WITH a piece of clotted blood on his forehead, and hand-cuffed to Police-Sergt. S. B. Williams, William John Dodds, the 50-year-old caretaker of Boxgrove School hostel, was led into Guildford Magistrates' Court at 12.30 on Wednesday.

Before Alderman Arthur Williams he was charged that he 'at Guildford in the County of Surrey on 22nd October, 1957, did murder Charles Barrett.' After evidence by Det.-Insp. D. Adams, Dodds was remanded in custody until Monday.

At an inquest on Wednesday afternoon, the cause of Mr. Barrett's death was stated to be a fractured skull and cerebral contusion (damage to the brain). The inquest was adjourned until December 18th.

Headline from the Surrey Advertiser. Surrey Advertiser

description of the two men seen fleeing the school, one towards Boxgrove Road, the other in the direction of Merrow Woods. Road blocks were set up so that the police could question car owners about anything suspicious they might have seen, watches were placed on bus and railway stations, police dogs searched the grounds of the school and officers conducted a house-to-house investigation. William Dodds, Alice Carr and Alan Byrne made official statements to the police.

When asked if he knew of anyone who might have had a reason to attack the old caretaker, Dodds replied, 'No, but he said something to me yesterday about a person whom he thought was hanging about the school.' When questioned about the weapon used against Barrett, Dodds could not be specific, but thought that it was probably made of metal judging from the noise it had made when it knocked against the wall as the man ran out of the boot hole. It was a twelve-year-old pupil who solved the mystery of the murder weapon. Charles Mills had been with some friends feeding the turkeys

MURDER CHARGE: 40 EXHIBITS IN COURT

Boy of 12 found a blood-stained coke shovel

A BLOOD-stained and battered coke shovel, which a 12-year-old boy said he had found, was produced at a special sitting of the Guildford borough magistrates on Wednesday. With it, alleged the prosecution, William John Dodds (50), assistant caretaker at Boxgrove School, Boxgrove Road, Guildford, murdered 67-year-old Mr. Charles Barrett, the resident caretaker, in the boot hole or cellar at the school on October 22nd.

In a statement read to the court Dodds was alleged to have said: "He (Mr. Barrett) was in a frightful temper and accused me of not doing by job properly . . . he hit me with a bunch of keys; I hit him with a torch . . . He lunged at me with a shovel and hit me . . . I wrestled that out of his hand . . . I reversed the shovel and hit him . . . I kept hitting him on the head; I lost my temper completely."

During the course of the hearing it was also alleged that Dodds may have hit Mr. Barrett with a rubber-cased torch and a small sandbag.

Headline from the Surrey Advertiser. Surrey Advertiser

that lived in the school grounds, when he found a battered and bloodstained spade near the dustbins.

During the course of the morning there was a reported sighting of one of the wanted men. He had allegedly been seen in the Clandon area, and the focus of the search turned in this direction. By midday no one had been found, and the search was again broadened.

Detective Inspector Adams spent a great deal of the afternoon at Guildford Police Station scrutinising the statement made by William Dodds. He was looking for some detail that would give them the edge in their search for the murderers, but as he read through he felt an intuitive unease; he decided to question Dodds further. Acting on instinct he tackled Dodds head on.

'After a lot of inquiries I find a lot of things you have told me in your statement don't appear correct.'

'I take it you have not found anybody,' was all Dodds replied.

The detective inspector pressed on with his hunch. 'No, we have not, and I don't think that they exist.'

'What I want to know is what will happen to my wife? I am worried about her.' Dodds was now becoming anxious and Detective Inspector Adams reminded him of the seriousness of the investigation and the need for absolute truth in his statement.

'Assuming that my story is wrong,' Dodds continued, 'there is only one charge anyway. If my story don't hang up, I hang anyway. Can my wife come here? She has always advised me what to do, and I am worried about her.'

William Dodds' wife was brought to the station and by a quarter past six in the evening Dodds asked to make another statement. The story, this time, was rather different. The *Surrey Advertiser* quoted from the parts of the statement that were read out at the hearing at Guildford Borough Magistrates' Court:

He [Barrett] *was in a frightful temper and accused me of not doing my job properly. I told him I was not doing his job … He shouted something about putting the torch off. He was really mad.*

He hit me with a bunch of keys around the fingers. I hit him with a torch; it is only rubber… He lunged at me with a shovel and hit me behind the left knee …I wrestled that out of his hand although he is pretty strong, taken all round. I reversed the shovel and hit him …I suddenly found him hitting me in the nose and face. I kept hitting him on the head; I lost my temper completely.

Dodds admitted that even after Alice Carr had interrupted them, he continued beating Charles Barrett over the head. So what was the history of the relationship between Dodds and Barrett that it should have come to such a violent end? Dodds had complained to the headmaster, Mr Evershed, on several occasions that Mr Barrett was making him work too hard, but the headmaster's view was that an assistant caretaker should be prepared to take instructions from the head caretaker, without interference from him. On the other hand, a gardener at the school, Richard Farmer, said that to all outward appearances Dodds and Barrett were the best of friends. Dodds had only recently begun his employment at the school, in fact in July of that year. The headmaster described Dodds as 'a very good, hard working man,' and added that he had

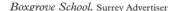

Boxgrove School. Surrey Advertiser

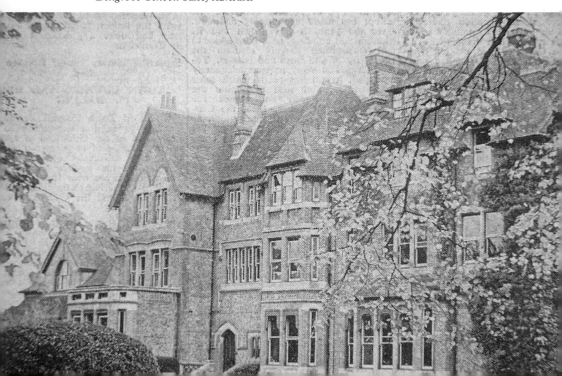

always liked him. Equally, he had never known Mr Barrett to be involved in any kind of quarrel in all his many years at the school, and he certainly had never known him to strike anyone. Was it a singular eruption of anger that led to the death of the sixty-seven-year-old caretaker?

More details emerged at the assize court trial in December 1957. In his evidence, Dodds stated that there had been tension between him and Barrett since the beginning of term in September. Dodds said that he had been asked by Barrett to clean the School Chapel, while Barrett and a farm hand unloaded the boys' trunks. Dealing with the luggage was always a favoured job since the parents would often tip the caretaker for carrying the large boxes. However, it was raining on the first day of this particular term and one of the teachers was concerned to see the sixty-seven-year-old struggling with the heavy cases and getting wet in the process. Dodds was called to take over from Barrett, and the older man was furious. He assumed that Dodds had requested the job in order to get the tips and warned him that he would get him sacked at the first opportunity. Dodds forestalled this, he said, by discussing the matter with the headmaster. It was during this discussion that Dodds later claimed the headmaster described Mr Barrett as 'cantankerous' and advised him that if he just held on for a year or so he would have Barrett's job. The headmaster denied ever having described Mr Barrett as 'cantankerous'.

On Tuesday, 22 October 1957 the argument between the two men flared up quickly. Barrett took pride in his punctuality, even setting his watch five minutes fast so that he would never be late. His normal routine was to wake at five o'clock in the morning, leave his house in the school grounds at six, carry out his early morning duties, such as lighting the oil burners, then return home for breakfast as seven so that he was ready to start the main part of his working day at nine. According to Dodds, on this particular day Barrett arrived slightly later than usual for work, and this was enough to set him in a bad frame of mind. Dodds arrived at the boot hole first and went to sort out his tools for the day. In his words, while he was doing this, 'I heard quite a patter of feet down the back steps leading to the boot hole and then the outer door burst open.' Mr Barrett shouted at Dodds, asking him why he had not seen to the oil burners or turned the lights on; these were tasks that the head caretaker normally did himself, and Dodds told him he was not about to do his work for him. The argument escalated. Heated words were exchanged and when Mr Barrett again told William Dodds that he was going to get him fired, Dodds laughed at him and told him that was not going to happen as he had already talked to the headmaster. This apparently tipped the older man in to a blaze of anger, and he allegedly lunged at Dodds, striking him with a set of keys. Dodds retaliated by hitting at him with the rubber torch that he happened to be holding, and that was when Barrett picked up the shovel. Twice he tried to hit Dodds with the spade, missing each time, before managing to hit him on the back of the legs at the third attempt. Dodds reached out to grab the first thing that came to hand and picked up a sandbag; he tried to hit Barrett with this but missed and instead decided to wrestle the spade from him. As Dodds explained at his trial:

He got madder. I tried to grab the shovel. We wrestled for it. I hit the handle of the shovel in his face. I took the shovel away from him by an army trick. I hit him again and again with the flat of the shovel, having reversed it on him.

When questioned by the judge, Dodds admitted that he had aimed his blows at the other man's head, even after Barrett fell on his face and had nothing with which to defend himself. The fight resumed after Alice Carr left to fetch the water because Charles Barrett grabbed at Dodds' feet, attempting to throw him off balance, and at this:

I lost my head completely then, my Lord. I do not know what I did after that. I just simply blacked out. I came to and found I was still hitting him. I was kneeling hitting him with the shovel.

Was he suggesting then, the prosecution wanted to know, that his actions were purely in self-defence? Dodds claimed that he was indeed acting to save his own life, even though the reality was that at that point Barrett was unarmed and injured and there was nothing to stop William Dodds from walking away from the boot hole.

There is only one version of the argument and the subsequent fight to inform us of the events of 22 October 1957; Charles Barrett was never able to put forward his side of the story. Even if we accept Dodds' version of provocation, does that in any way justify the violence used on the caretaker by a man seventeen years his junior? Interestingly, at the assize court hearing Barrett's wife, Gladys, revealed that her husband 'had been getting rather shaky on his legs' recently. The pathologist who examined Charles Barrett's body, Dr Arthur Mant, discovered two types of injury to his head; the first appeared to have been made by a blunt but reasonably heavy instrument, possibly the rubber torch, and the second by a lighter but sturdy weapon, most likely the spade. But it was the pathologist's opinion that if these were in fact the murder weapons, then a considerable amount of force would have been needed to inflict such extensive injuries.

On the other hand, when Dodds' injuries were examined they were found to be very superficial. He had various abrasions on the face, plausibly caused by a bunch of keys, a bruise to the elbow and another behind the left knee, which is where Dodds claimed that Barrett had hit him with the shovel. He complained of further bruises to the buttocks and hips but no marks were visible. Even if the fight were justified, it was certainly unevenly matched.

William Dodds' counsel asked for the charge to be reduced to manslaughter on the grounds of extreme provocation. For this to be acceptable to the court, defence counsel would need to demonstrate that the provocation was such that it would deprive any reasonable person of all self-control. The judge, Mr Justice Hilbery, felt that, based on the evidence, it did not apply in this case. In only seven minutes the jury found William Dodds guilty of the murder of Charles Barrett, and Mr Justice Hilbery duly passed sentence on him:

By virtue of the provisions of the Homicide Act 1957, there is only one sentence which is the sentence of the law in these circumstances, as it is not a capital murder, that is you be imprisoned for life.

Dodds had been mistaken in believing, on the day of his arrest, that he was doomed to be hanged, since by this time the crime of murder had been separated into two distinct categories; murder and capital murder. He had been charged with the former and it was only capital murder that now carried the death penalty.

Select Bibliography

Anglo-Saxon Chronicle

Barlow, Frank *The Godwins* (2002)

Blair, P H *An Introduction to Anglo-Saxon England* (1959)

Campbell, Alistair (ed.) *Encomium Emmae Reginae* (1949 edition)

Chouler, W H *Tales of Old Surrey* (1985)

Critchley, Macdonald *The Trial of August Sangret* (1959)

Dickens, Charles *A December Vision: His Social Journalism* (1986 edition)

Dickens, Charles *Nicholas Nickleby* (1839)

Guildford Jackdaw

Harrison, J F C *Early Victorian Britain, 1832–51* (1988)

Hewins, Judy *The Hindhead Murder 1786-1986* (1986)

Higham, N J *The Death of Anglo-Saxon England* (2000)

Humble, Richard *The Fall of Saxon England* (1975)

Janaway, John *Surrey Murders* (1988)

Johnson W H *Surrey Murder Casebook* (2000)

Johnson W H *Surrey Tales of Mystery and Murder* (2002)

Lawson, M K *Cnut: The Danes in England* (1993)

Malmesbury, William of *The Kings Before the Norman Conquest* (translated from Latin 1989)

Moorey, Peter *Who Was The Sailor Murdered at Hindhead?* (2000)

Newgate Calendar (1932 edition)

Pritchard, R E *Dicken's England: Life in Victorian Times* (2002)

Roberts, Tom *Friends and Villains: An Autobiography* (1987)

Stafford, Pauline *Queen Emma and Queen Edith* (1997)

Stenton, Sir Frank *Anglo-Saxon England* (1971)

Trial of Chennell and Chalcraft for the Horrid Murders at Godalming Anon (1818)

Triggs, T *The Saxons* (1979)

Trow, M J *The Wigwam Murder* (1994)

Whitlock, Ralph *The Warrior Kings of Saxon England* (1997)

Wilson, David *The Anglo-Saxons* (1971)

Wojtczak, Helena *Women of Victorian Sussex* (2003)

Wood, Tim *The Saxons and The Normans* (1989)

Wright, Thomas *Hindhead or the English Switzerland* (1898)

Index